D1324718

British Airways

Third Edition

Leo Marriott

Ian Allan
PUBLISHING

Contents

First published 1993
Second edition 1997
Third edition 2000

ISBN 0 7110 2716 1

Published by Ian Allan Publishing
an imprint of Ian Allan Publishing Ltd,
Terminal House, Shepperton, Surrey TW17 8AS.
Printed by Ian Allan Printing Ltd, Riverdene
Business Park, Hersham, Surrey KT12 4RG.

Code: 0005/D

Front cover: **British Airways 767-336 (ER), G-BNWV.** *Austin J. Brown/ Aviation Picture Library*

Back cover: **Concorde entered service in 1976.** *Malcolm Bradbury*

Title page: **Chelsea Rose.** *Author*

Below left: **Union Flag — the new image of British Airways.** *Robbie Shaw*

Below right: **Lining up for the Millennium.** *Malcolm Bradbury*

Introduction

Left: **Concorde — still the pride of the fleet!**
Malcolm Bradbury

British Airways enters the new millennium in a state of considerable flux. It has now been in existence for over a quarter of a century following its establishment as Britain's major flag carrier in 1974 and, while change is inevitable over such a timescale, the pace has undoubtedly quickened in the last few years. At the time of its formation, the airline industry was run in a very traditional and conservative manner, with most countries having a state-owned national carrier and any independents having to fight hard to compete against cosy monopolies or rigid pool arrangements.

Today, this has changed completely. Over the last two decades, a trend towards privatisation has gathered momentum, with British Airways being one of the earliest examples involving a state-owned airline. A parallel trend in the spread of deregulated domestic and international services has resulted in the survival of the larger and better managed airlines, generally at the expense of smaller and inefficient operators. This has been coupled with the sophisticated application of computerised booking and ticketing services by third party agencies, in which one or more airlines can integrate their route networks to avoid duplication, and share booking codes so that the passenger appears to receive a seamless service around the world. Such co-operation, often the cause of bitter controversy, has grown from simple code-sharing of flight numbers to strong affiliations and groupings in

which passenger services, loyalty schemes, ground handling, ticketing and reservations, and many other aspects of day-to-day operations are conducted to a common standard. At present the airlines involved maintain their own identities, although in some cases technical aspects such as aircraft servicing are centralised and even the selection and purchase of aircraft can be synchronised. Inevitably, in time to come, this will lead to the formation of a few supra-national mega carriers who will carry the great majority of the world's commercial traffic.

Against this background, British Airways has a number of strategies to ensure that it remains a major player on the world stage. To counter the powerful Star Alliance which includes airlines such as United Airlines, Lufthansa, SAS, Air Canada and Thai Airways, it was instrumental in the setting up of the **one**world™ concept in partnership with American Airlines, QANTAS, Canadian Airlines and Cathay Pacific. In addition, it is gradually spreading its share of regional markets either by setting up new airlines, buying existing operators or by means of a franchise agreement with existing carriers. In this way airlines flying in British Airways' colours now exist in France, Holland, Denmark, Italy and South Africa. Within the United Kingdom, subsidiary and franchise airlines, including Brymon Airways, CityFlyer Express and British Regional Airlines, have taken over many of the domestic and European routes. At the same time a brand-new, low-fare, no-frills operation known as Go was set up in 1997 to counteract the increasing success of new airlines such as EasyJet and Ryanair which had successfully tapped a new market of budget-conscious travellers.

These innovations, many introduced in the three years since the last edition of this book was published in 1998, have led logically to a major realignment of the core British Airways strategy. This will now be directed at the higher-yield business passenger as the subsidiary and franchise operators increasingly take care of the leisure and economy end of the market and become responsible for low-density routes which do not suit the larger aircraft on the mainline fleet. The results of this are beginning to become apparent in the make-up of the British Airways' mainline fleet where many older aircraft such as the DC-10 and early versions of the Boeing 747 have been retired and are being replaced with the versatile twin-engined Boeing 777. Even the Boeing 757, for many years the backbone of the European and domestic services, is now scheduled to be withdrawn over the next few years in favour of the smaller Airbus A320 and A319. The Boeing 767 fleet is also due to be reduced.

In 1997 British Airways unveiled a brave new image to the world but somehow the intended message was blurred and the new multi-ethnic livery was not a great success, at least not in its home countries. Today, in the face of much adverse criticism, the airline has returned to its British roots and the Union Flag now flies proudly on the tails of many of its aircraft. The changes in the composition of its fleet outlined above are in reaction to strong competition and falling profit margins. After many years of impressive financial performance backed up by a public relations profile the envy of many other airlines, British Airways is now going through a difficult time as we enter a new millennium. However, it should not be forgotten that, despite all the problems, British Airways and its direct subsidiaries and franchise operators together form the fourth-busiest airline group in the world. There is plenty to build on and the years ahead will hopefully allow the airline to see the benefit of the major reorganisation currently in progress and once again be able to lay claim to being the 'World's Favourite Airline'.

Above: **Imperial Airways was formed in 1924 and was an early predecessor of British Airways. Shown here is G-EBMY, one of nine de Havilland DH-66s used on mail services to the Middle East and Africa between 1926 and 1935.** *Winged Memories/BAe*

Top right: **Formed in 1946, the state-owned British European Airways was initially based at Northolt where this early photograph was taken.** *Author's Collection*

British Airways - A Brief History

In simple terms British Airways was formed by the merger of its famous predecessors, British Overseas Airways Corporation (BOAC) and British European Airways (BEA), and operations under the new title formally commenced in April 1974. However, this momentous event was the culmination of many years' work going back to the 1960s when the government gave considerable thought to the problems and future shape of the British airline industry. In May 1969 the result of a formal government inquiry was published in the Edwards Report which recommended the establishment of a British Airways Board to oversee the activities of BOAC, BEA and British Air Services (BAS) and also to encourage the growth of a 'second force' independent airline in which the board would also hold a share. At this stage it was expected that BOAC and BEA would continue to operate as separate airlines but there was considerable political pressure for a full merger. Following the provisions of the Civil Aviation Act (1971), the new British Airways Board was established on 1 April 1972 and took over control of the assets of the two airlines. One of its first actions was to reorganise the airlines into seven operating divisions which became effective as from 1 September 1972. These were:

BOAC Division: Effectively all operational aspects of the long-haul airline.
BEA Division: The operational part of the short-haul airline and subdivided into Mainline, Super 1-11, Cargo and Airtours divisions.
BAS Division: The former British Air Services regional fleets of Cambrian, Northeast, Scottish and Channel.
British Airways Helicopters: The former BEA Helicopters.
British Airways Engineering: Engine overhaul based on the established BOAC facility at Treforest, Wales.
British Airways Associate Companies: Incorporating the various associate and subsidiary companies such as hotel and tour groups formerly owned by BEA and BOAC.
International Air Radio: A jointly owned company originally set up to provide ATC services and communications networks required by the airlines.

Following on from this reorganisation, the board also recommended that the single name 'British Airways' be adopted to cover the activities of the seven divisions and this title was formally adopted on 1 September 1973. The last recommendation, made in November 1972, proposed the long-expected total merger of the airlines and this was accepted without delay by the government so that British Airways was finally born, after a long gestation, on 1 April 1974.

In considering the story of British Airways it is relevant to look briefly at the history of BEA and BOAC, the two state-owned corporations set up during and after World War 2 and

Above: **BEA was closely involved in the design of the Hawker Siddeley Trident which entered service in 1964 and subsequently served British Airways until 1985.** *Author's Collection*

Below: **BOAC ordered its first Boeing 747s in 1966 and began commercial services in 1971. The aircraft subsequently formed the backbone of British Airways' long-haul fleet after its formation in 1974.** *Author's Collection/BOAC*

Bottom: **Take-off! The complex process of forming British Airways was completed in April 1974.** *Rolls-Royce*

themselves the result of government-inspired mergers. BOAC was formed in 1940 as a result of the nationalisation and combining of Imperial Airways and the original British Airways. Of the two, Imperial was the older, having been formed in 1924 from the amalgamation of several smaller airlines, and was also the larger. Its fleet of aircraft, including the magnificent C Class flying boats, flew services around the world providing vital links throughout the British Empire which was then at its zenith. British Airways was more of a newcomer, having been formed in 1935 from the merger of Hillman's Airways, Spartan Air Lines, and United Airlines, and its main base was at Heston — just north of the present Heathrow. After World War 2 BOAC concentrated on the rebuilding of its long-haul services and a new state-owned corporation, BEA, was established on 1 August 1946 to operate domestic and European flights. There was also a third state-owned airline, British South American Airways (BSAA), which was set up to operate services to South America and the Caribbean using a fleet of Avro Tudors, but operations ceased in 1949 after the unexplained loss of two aircraft. Initially, BEA took over European transport and passenger flights which had been flown by the RAF from the closing stages of the war but in 1947 a large number of independent airlines were nationalised and their aircraft and routes absorbed into BEA.

In the 1950s both airlines expanded considerably and were responsible for many pioneering innovations in the field of civil air transport. After experience with a converted DC-3 powered by Rolls-Royce Dart turboprops, BEA went on to become the world's first airline to fly regular scheduled services with turboprop airliners when the first world-beating Viscounts were delivered in 1953. In the meantime BOAC was blazing a trail with the world's first jet airliner, the de Havilland Comet, with passenger services commencing in 1952. Unfortunately, a series of tragic accidents led to its grounding in 1954 and jet services did not recommence until 1958 when the much-improved Comet IV entered service and BOAC regained some of its lost prestige by being the first airline to fly transatlantic jet services in October of that year, beating Pan American by three weeks.

Despite many attempts by the British aircraft industry to meet BOAC's requirements, the airline generally ended up ordering American equipment for its long-range fleet. Thus Stratocruisers, Constellations and DC-7Cs outlasted the British-built Hermes in the 1950s, and Comets and Britannias were later replaced by Boeing 707s. In 1964 the British Vickers VC10 entered service, followed by the stretched Super VC10 in 1965, and this latter version was probably superior to the 707 in almost every respect but did not attract enough orders to be a commercial success. By comparison, BEA adopted a staunch 'Buy British' policy and rapidly moved from piston-engined DC-3s and Elizabethans on to the turboprop Viscount and its successor, the Vanguard. These were followed in 1960 by the short/medium-range Comet 4B and the specially designed Trident in 1964. In 1966 the airline ordered a fleet of BAC111-500s for use on its German services from Berlin and for regional services from Manchester. BEA's last significant order prior to the formation of British Airways was for up to 18 Rolls-Royce-powered Lockheed L-1011 TriStars, although the first of these was not delivered until 1975 when it appeared in British Airways' markings. (The airline's first choice had been the projected BAC311 but this did not go ahead due to a lack of government support.)

In the late 1960s BOAC initiated orders for two aircraft types which were to play a significant role in the developing fortunes of the modern British Airways. The first of these was the Anglo-French Concorde. BOAC was closely involved in its development and the aircraft first flew in prototype form in 1969 although passenger-carrying services did not commence until 1976, and then under British Airways' colours. The other was, of course, the wide-bodied Boeing 747 which was to revolutionise the economics of long-haul airline operations. BOAC's initial order was placed in 1966 and deliveries began in 1970 with no less than 15 being in service when British Airways took over in 1974.

After the formation of British Airways in 1974, the original seven operating divisions continued to exist and were joined by two additional organisations responsible for passenger product sales (British Airways Travel Division) and cargo handling and sales (British Airways Cargo UK).

Above: **British Airtours was the airline's charter subsidiary.** *Ian MacFarlane*

Left: **BEA's helicopter operations continued under the title British Airways Helicopters until this subsidiary was sold to the Maxwell Group in 1986 and became British Independent Helicopters, still in existence today after further changes of ownership.**
British Airports Authority

At this time the airline had a fleet of around 215 aircraft and employed over 58,000 staff and, from an operational point of view, was still run as two separate airlines. However, in 1977 a fundamental reorganisation was carried out with the aim of achieving more integration and centralised control. The previous Overseas, European and Regional Divisions were combined into a single unified operating structure with centralised departments responsible for commercial operations, flight operations, engineering, planning, catering, personnel and other services. Airline operations were organised into six (later reduced to five) separate route structures, three long-haul, two European and one domestic. British Airtours continued as the charter subsidiary and British Airways Helicopters also retained its autonomy.

In the meantime, there had been exciting developments on the commercial side with the

first European shuttle operation having been inaugurated in 1975 on the Heathrow-Glasgow route. Pioneered in the United States, the shuttle concept introduced the idea of high-frequency flights on busy routes using simplified ticketing procedures with seat availability guaranteed by the use of standby aircraft. The instant success of this operation led to its adoption on the London-Edinburgh service in 1976 and subsequently to other domestic routes. In the same year British Airways, jointly with Air France, became the first airline to offer supersonic passenger services with Concorde flights to Washington and the Middle East.

On the domestic front, British Airways was giving serious thought in 1981 to closing down the loss-making Glasgow-based Highlands and Islands services and handing the routes over to smaller airlines. However, a staff proposal which involved significant staff cuts and re-equipping with HS748s was accepted and a new autonomous Highlands Division was set up and was consistently profitable until most of its routes were taken over by British Regional Airlines. A similar situation occurred at Birmingham where, again, the enthusiasm of local staff was responsible for keeping services in place. In 1982 there was further rationalisation and reorganisation of all other operations which were now divided between three new self-contained divisions — Intercontinental (long-haul flights), European (combining all domestic and short-haul flights) and Gatwick Services. The latter was responsible for all British Airways flights operating from Gatwick, including those of British Airtours whose main base was at the airport. As a result of this reorganisation and the steady elimination of duplicated resources stemming from the original structure inherited from BEA and BOAC, British Airways staff numbers had fallen dramatically by this time to around 35,000. In 1983, while retaining the three flight operations divisions, the commercial and accounting network was broken up into eight self-contained route centres.

British Airways Helicopters, which had continued as a self-contained operation since the 1974 merger, was sold off in 1986 to the Mirror Newspaper Group to become British Independent Helicopters. This sale, and the earlier airline reorganisations, were among many measures taken in the mid-1980s in preparation for the privatisation of British Airways which took place in February 1987 when the sale of 720 million shares raised a total of £900 million. Freed from the restraints of state control, the airline immediately began a programme of expansion and acquisition ultimately aimed at turning it into a world force. In July 1987 it made a surprise bid for the entire share capital of rival independent British Caledonian and, after much hard bargaining with the Monopolies Commission and other interested parties, the deal was finalised by the end of the year. BCAL's fleet of five Boeing 747-200s, 8 DC-10-30s and 13 BAC111-500s was quickly absorbed and repainted, although the General Electric-powered 747s were not retained as they were not compatible with BA's Rolls-Royce-powered fleet. In addition, British Airways also took over a BCAL order for 10

Airbus A320s which became the airline's first and, for many years, only Airbus type.

In the wake of the BCAL take-over, British Airways' Gatwick operations were substantially enlarged and reorganised with a fleet of 14 Boeing 737s and a number of long-haul aircraft. The charter subsidiary, British Airtours, was renamed Caledonian and adopted a new livery based on the previous BCAL colours, retaining the distinctive tartan uniforms for the cabin crews. Also, in 1988, all British Airways activities were transferred to Gatwick's newly opened North Terminal which offered much-improved passenger facilities. In the wake of the downturn in traffic experienced after the Gulf War, plans were announced in January 1992 to reorganise operations at Gatwick by means of revised schedules calculated to appeal to business travellers, together with various moves intended to reduce costs and improve efficiency. These plans received a considerable boost following the take-over of rival independent Dan Air in October 1992 with the addition of several new scheduled routes and the acquisition of a fleet of modern Boeing 737-300/400 aircraft. British Airways then proceeded to set up a new low-cost, short-haul operation based on the merging of its own and Dan Air's former Gatwick scheduled routes which has resulted in a network serving 56 destinations in 31 countries with over 400 flights a week. This is now organised as a separate division under the title British Airways (European Operations) and has its own dedicated fleet of Boeing 737s and 757s.

Although scheduled operations from Gatwick have increased substantially, a policy decision to withdraw from the unpredictable inclusive tour market resulted in the sale of Caledonian Airways to the Inspirations travel group at the end of 1994 for the sum of £16.6 million. During its last year as part of the British Airways group, Caledonian had carried over 2.2 million passengers and continued to operate successfully after being transferred to its new owners on 1 April 1995. Ownership changed again in 1997 when it became part of the Carlton Leisure Group. However, a major shake-down in the UK travel industry in 1999 led to Caledonian being merged with the IT (or 'charter') airline Flying Colours and the resulting airline was renamed JMC Airlines for the 2000

Left: **Overseas acquisitions began in 1992 with the German airline Delta Air Regionalflugverkehr. This was quickly transformed into an all-jet operator and renamed Deutsche BA.** *Author*

Left: **Today British Airways is more than just an airline. It is a network of partners and subsidiaries strategically placed to provide a seamless worldwide network.** *Author*

season, thus bringing an illustrious name in British aviation to an end.

The setting up of a European Division at Gatwick fitted well with the reorganisation of regional scheduled services which had taken place a few months earlier in 1992. This resulted in a new subsidiary company, BA Regional, which was formed to operate regional services from Birmingham, Manchester and Glasgow. One immediate result was the withdrawal of the long-serving BAC111s previously based at Manchester and Birmingham and their replacement by Boeing 737-200s carrying the new Regional title. The Scottish services were operated by a fleet of 13 new British Aerospace ATPs which replaced the BAe748s previously used. In addition to flying domestic and European services from the regional centres, the new subsidiary also operated some transatlantic services which commenced in 1993 and used Boeing 757s and 767s leased from the parent company, although these long-haul routes have had patchy success and have been withdrawn

on occasions.

Even with this new regional organisation in place, there were still many low-density, short-haul domestic and European routes which could not be operated economically by Boeing 737s, or even in some cases by the 64-seater ATPs. In order to fill this gap, and to gain additional feeder traffic to boost medium and long-haul routes from major traffic, the concept of the British Airways Express franchise system was born. Under this scheme, small airlines would adopt British Airways' livery and their crews would wear British Airways uniforms. Operating and customer service standards would be closely monitored to ensure that British Airways' standards were maintained but the airline would remain independent, although BA would also assist with marketing, reservations and ticketing systems. There were advantages for both sides in this arrangement. The franchisee bought into the British Airways image with its invaluable marketing advantages while British Airways itself could effectively have various routes operated at no cost to itself and gained considerably in additional interline traffic. The first airline to participate in this scheme was Gatwick-based CityFlyer Express in August 1993 and it was later followed by Loganair, Manx European (a forerunner of British Regional Airlines) and Brymon Airways. Subsequently, airlines such as GB Airways and British Mediterranean Airlines also joined the franchise scheme, while overseas operators began to take an interest in aligning themselves with British Airways. In these circumstances, the title British Airways Express, with its commuter connotations, was no longer appropriate and it was quietly dropped. Franchise airlines now carry standard British Airways livery and are virtually indistinguishable from the parent company's aircraft except for a small company logo on the forward fuselage.

In the early 1990s British Airways was set firmly on the acquisition trail and had not only British airlines in its sights. Initially it received several setbacks and a bid to take a shareholding in Sabena was rejected in 1991 while a proposed merger with Dutch carrier KLM also fell through. However, in mid-1992 it took a 51% shareholding in Delta Air Regionalflugverkehr, a small German airline which was subsequently named Deutsche BA and became wholly owned in 1998. Also in 1992, British Airways took a substantial shareholding in Transport Aérien Transrégional (TAT), which was converted to full ownership in 1997, while in 1996 it bought another French airline, Air Liberté, which it subsequently merged with TAT. These purchases gave British Airways a strong foothold in continental Europe which was strengthened by franchise agreements with Sun Air of Scandinavia and BASE Airlines in Holland. The most recent enterprise, due to become operational, is a start-up airline in Italy to be called Italia BA.

At home, many of British Airways' domestic and European routes were being hit by competition from new low-cost airlines such as Ryanair and EasyJet. Low overheads enabled these operators to offer fares at a level which British Airways had no hope of directly matching and, in any case, would not offer much financial return even if it could. However, BA was determined to compete in this end of the market and very quickly set up its own low-cost airline

at Stansted which began operating in May 1998. Planned in secret under the code name 'Blue Sky', the new airline rejoiced in the simple name Go. Now in its second year of operation, it is performing strongly but is yet to show a profit. One of its original competitors, Debonair, has ceased trading, but there is still considerable competition, not least from the KLM-backed Buzz which will also fly from Stansted.

Although these arrangements did much to expand British Airways' commercial empire, it was the long and medium-haul routes from London which were the core of the airline's business. In this field, the acquisition of a major airline was unlikely and so various attempts were made to take partial shareholdings or to establish broad-ranging code-sharing agreements. A start was made in 1988 when a marketing agreement was made with United Airlines giving BA passengers access to a major US domestic network. An offer to buy out United was rejected by the US government and the agreement subsequently lapsed. Opposition also led to the withdrawal at the end of 1992 of a bid for 49% of US Air although British Airways subsequently negotiated a 24.6% shareholding which was approved in May 1993, leading to close co-operation between the two airlines. As a result, the airlines entered into a code-sharing agreement and some services from Gatwick to the US were flown by US Air aircraft painted in BA colours with their crews wearing BA uniforms and applying the British airline's standards of service. Despite the injection of capital from British Airways, US Air continued to have financial problems until very recently and the alliance was not a happy one, being formally dissolved in 1997 when British Airways sold its shareholding. Part of the reason for this was a proposed formal alliance and partnership between British Airways and American Airlines. Had this been implemented as desired, it would have put the two airlines in a commanding position on the lucrative North Atlantic route and for that reason has been continually opposed by other carriers who forced the merger plans to be scrutinised by various bodies including the US Department of Transport and the European Commission. Ultimately, the conditions set by the Commission for its approval of the alliance have proved unacceptable and to date it has not been implemented although, as will be seen, the two airlines have maintained a close working relationship.

On the other side of the world, in 1992 British Airways successfully bid for a 25% stake in QANTAS, the Australian national airline. Since that date there has been close co-operation on the so-called 'kangaroo route' between London and Australia with up to 28 flights a week now available from the two carriers and a choice of intermediate stopovers in Kuala Lumpur, Singapore or Bangkok. Even more flexibility is possible as passengers can fly British Airways to Paris and then on to Australia on a direct QANTAS flight using a single ticket. Another attempt to set up an international alliance occurred following the break-up of the former USSR when British Airways was involved in the start-up of a new airline, Air Russia. This was to be a joint venture with Aeroflot in which services were expected to commence in 1994. Although this project did not reach fruition, British Airways was subsequently involved in training programmes with several CIS airlines to assist them to bring their service, maintenance and operations up to western standards.

The lack of official approval for the alliance with American Airlines was a serious matter in the late 1990s as other airlines began to form wide-ranging global alliances and British Airways was in danger of being left out on a limb. The company was, therefore, instrumental in helping to form a new alliance under the brand name **one**world™. As well as British Airways and American Airlines, the founder members were QANTAS, Canadian Airlines and Cathay Pacific. From early 1999 these airlines operated a sophisticated code-sharing system as well as standardising levels of service and sharing frequent-flyer incentive schemes. By the end of the year they had been joined by Finnair and Iberia, with BA taking a 9% shareholding in the latter, while LAN Chile was expected to join in 2000.

The international air transport business is one of the most competitive in the world and it is increasingly obvious that only the largest and most efficient will survive. Consequently, there is continuing pressure on British Airways' management to make the airline ever more efficient and productive. Some time ago the then chairman, Robert Ayling, talked about the concept of a 'virtual airline' which would contract out many services such as accounting, passenger handling, maintenance and training. It would not even own its aircraft and premises but lease them from other agencies, leaving only a core of essential staff and management services actually working directly for the airline. Although this seemed far-fetched only two or three years ago, all the signs are that it will happen to some extent in the early part of the 21st century. Already many domestic and short-haul services have been delegated to subsidiaries and franchise operators and the signs are that this practice will increase. Many of the aircraft in the core long-haul fleet are not fully owned by British Airways but are the subject of complex leasing and finance deals. Some of the long-haul services flown from Gatwick using Boeing 777s are actually operated by a paper airline called Airline Management Limited in which the crews and cabin services are provided by a third party. Large sections of ground handling, administration, engineering, catering and other support services are contracted out and inevitably this process is set to continue. British Airways has now existed for a quarter of a century and it is already substantially different from the company which was established in 1974. It therefore remains the subject of speculation as to what will be the nature and structure of British Airways at the end of its second quarter century. Almost anything is possible: it may be a major world brand or it may have disappeared completely, absorbed into some mega world airline. Only time will tell, but the time ahead will certainly be interesting and challenging.

2. A World Airline

As the structure of British Airways changes and it increasingly operates in partnership with subsidiaries, franchisees and allied airlines, it is not always apparent as to who is the true operator of a particular aircraft or service. In this chapter all the operational components which come together with British Airways to provide passenger services are briefly described and set in context. These include the operating divisions of British Airways itself, subsidiaries in which British Airways is the sole or major shareholder, and franchise operators. In almost every case aircraft flown by operators in these categories are finished in British Airways livery. Brief details are also given of airlines in which British Airways has a minority shareholding or which are involved in a formal alliance or code-sharing agreement. In these cases the aircraft operate in the colours of their parent airline.

Below: **The British Airways European Operation at Gatwick was formed following the take-over of Dan Air in 1992. G-BVNM, shown here, was one of several Boeing 737s acquired in this way.** *Mike Barth*

British Airways Operating Divisions

This section covers those divisions and organisations which are an integral part of the British Airways operation. Effectively these can be regarded as the constituent components of the airline.

British Airways Mainline Fleet

This is the core of British Airways' passenger operations and includes most of the aircraft based at London Heathrow as well as some long and medium-haul aircraft at Gatwick. It includes all of the Boeing 747 fleet as well as a substantial portion of the newer 777 fleet. Based at Heathrow is the flagship Concorde fleet and the majority of the long-haul fleet. In addition, Boeing 767s and 757s operate a substantial range of services on high-density European routes, while the latter also maintain the important super shuttle services to Manchester, Glasgow, Edinburgh and Belfast. Boeing 737-400s operate mainly on some less busy European routes or provide off-peak services on the busier routes. Finally, there are

Below left: **British Airways Regional was formed in 1992 to operate services from various regional centres. Originally the aircraft carried the name of their base airport alongside the British Airways title as shown on this Boeing 737 at Birmingham.** *Author*

the 10 Airbus A320s flying domestic and European services. At Gatwick, aircraft of the mainline fleet operate some long-haul services using Boeing 777s, 767s and 747s, notably to Africa, the Caribbean, Mexico and the southern United States. For operational, training and administrative purposes these aircraft are organised in fleets by type, each with a Fleet Captain, although for convenience the small A320 fleet is currently combined with the Boeing 737 fleet. However, this will probably change as the recently ordered A320 family aircraft begin to arrive. Also, the Boeing 757s and 767s form a single fleet with the added advantage of a common type rating for pilots, allowing them to be deployed between the two types. In the year ended March 1999, Mainline scheduled services carried just over 37 million passengers with a load factor of 70.7% and also carried 855,000 tonnes of cargo. The total unduplicated route distance was 426,000 statute miles (686,000km).

British Airways (European Operations at Gatwick)

Under this rather cumbersome and formal title, British Airways set up a substantial scheduled service operation at Gatwick following its take-over of the independent Dan Air in late 1992. More commonly referred to as British Airways (European), it was originally built around the fleet of Boeing 737-300s and -400s acquired from Dan Air, and then expanded by the allocation of more 737s (200s and 400s) transferred from Heathrow. The range of destinations served from Gatwick rose steadily as British Airways transferred many services from Heathrow so that more landing slots at the larger airport could be allocated to premium long-haul flights. As traffic continued to expand, larger aircraft including Boeing 757s and 767s were allocated to the Gatwick operation. Although British Airways maintains substantial overhaul and maintenance facilities at Gatwick, there is a constant rotation of aircraft between the various operating divisions.

British Airways Regional

This operating division of British Airways was set up in 1992 to run services from the major regional airports at Birmingham, Manchester

and Glasgow. A fleet of BAC111s was already in place at the two English airports but these were rapidly replaced by more modern Boeing 737-236s released from the Mainline fleet as they, in turn, were replaced by deliveries of the larger and quieter Boeing 737-436. In Scotland the original Highland Division Hawker Siddeley 748s were replaced by the larger British Aerospace ATP but, in 1994, the BA Regional Division ceased to have responsibility for regional services from Glasgow and these were taken over by Manx European and Loganair under the franchise scheme. In the meantime, BA Regional concentrated on building up substantial route networks from Manchester and Birmingham, and some of these included long-haul services, usually to New York using Boeing 757s or 767s leased for the purpose from the Mainline fleet. In recent years the replacement of the Boeing 737-236s, some of which are almost 20 years old, assumed some urgency as these aircraft would not be able to fly to most airports in Europe after 2002 due to Chapter 3 noise limitations. At the end of 1998 it was announced that the requirement for new aircraft would be met by variants of the very successful Airbus A320 and the first aircraft, an A319, was delivered to Birmingham in October 1999. The last of the Boeing 737s will be retired by 2001 and the Airbus fleet is being built up. Prior to the introduction of the current livery, BA Regional aircraft carried the titles British Airways Birmingham or British Airways Manchester, depending on where they were based. However, all aircraft now carry only the standard British Airways logo and lettering. Both British Airways Regional and British Airways (European) are run as entirely independent divisions within the British Airways structure and are responsible for their own financial management.

British Asia Airlines

British Asia Airlines is a Heathrow-based operating subsidiary, created in 1993 to operate services to Taipei, the capital of Taiwan. The fleet consists of two Boeing 747-436s (currently G-CIVA and G-CIVB) painted in basic British Airways Utopia livery with British Asia Airways logos and titles. As British Airways already flew to Beijing, the capital of mainland China, the

Above: **Regional carrier Brymon Airways became a wholly-owned subsidiary of British Airways in 1993 following the break-up of the short-lived Brymon European venture. It currently operates a substantial number of Bombardier Dash 8s and these will shortly be joined by regional jets in the shape of the Embraer ERJ-145.** *Author*

new airline was partly financed by Taiwan business interests as political pressures prevent any single carrier operating services to both mainland China and Taiwan.

Airline Management Limited (AML)

This is effectively a paper airline which flies three Boeing 777s modified to a high-density seating arrangement for services to the Caribbean and Mexico area from London Gatwick. The aircraft are owned by British Airways and painted in BA colours but are flown by crews provided by the independent airline Flying Colours (now JMC Airlines). It was originally set up to operate long-haul services from Gatwick using British Airways DC-10s but the last of these was retired in early 1999.

British Airways Subsidiaries

In the immediate aftermath of privatisation, British Airways expanded its operations by direct take-overs of airlines such as British Caledonian in 1987 and Dan Air in 1992. In each case the airline concerned was completely absorbed and any trace of its identity was lost. However, over the years British Airways has also taken over or acquired major shareholdings in various airlines, both British and European, which have been allowed to retain their individual operating status while still adopting the parent airline's standards and

market image. In each case the airline is financially independent and responsible for all aspects of its operation. These airlines are described here, together with Go Fly, which is also a wholly owned subsidiary but was set up specifically by British Airways in response to a market requirement.

Brymon Airways

Brymon Airways has had a chequered history but is now firmly established as a wholly owned British Airways subsidiary operating a variety of regional services. It began operations in 1972 with an Islander aircraft flying services between Newquay and the Isles of Scilly. British Airways first took a share in Brymon around 1980 when the airline began a steady expansion of services from its Plymouth base and was the first UK operator to acquire the DHC-7 with its spectacular STOL performance. In 1981 Brymon became involved in oil contract services based in Aberdeen, flying industry workers to Unst and other island destinations, and during the 1980s a Shorts 330 was acquired for a brief period to operate a Birmingham-Gatwick service as part of the BCAL Commuter network. The Dash 7s were put to good use in the development of London City Airport where the airline began operations in October 1987. Continuing its association with De Havilland Canada, Brymon became the first UK airline to fly the twin-engined Dash 8 in 1990 when it took delivery of two 100 series aircraft. In the meantime, the ownership of

Above: **Gatwick-based CityFlyer became a wholly-owned British Airways subsidiary in 1999, but prior to that it was the first airline to adopt the British Airways Express franchise, in 1993. It currently flies ATR turboprops and Avro RJs, one of which is shown here In the now standard Union Flag livery.** *British Aerospace*

Brymon was vested in a company called TPL (The Plimsol Line) of which British Airways and Maersk, a Danish transport conglomerate, each held a 40% shareholding. TPL also owned Birmingham European Airways and it was decided to merge the two companies in October 1992, under the title Brymon European. The Brymon fleet was briefly repainted in a new livery but, within 12 months, the merger was dissolved and Brymon reverted to its original title, although it was now 100% owned by British Airways, and the aircraft adopted BA livery from late 1993 onwards. In January 1995 it adopted even closer ties, formally becoming a British Airways Express operator although this title was subsequently dropped and all Brymon aircraft now carry the standard British Airways logo. Early in 1996 it was announced that most of its Dash 7s and Dash 8-100s would be replaced by the new Dash 8-300 series, a total of nine aircraft eventually being delivered. Two Dash 7s were retained for oil industry support operations in Scotland, wearing a new house livery and not BA colours. In 1998 Brymon placed a £60 million order for eight Dash 8Q-300s featuring an active noise suppression system claimed to give the smoothest and quietest ride of any current turboprop passenger aircraft. These had all been delivered by early 1999 when the Brymon fleet

numbered no less than 17 Dash 8s. To meet a requirement for further expansion, the airline evaluated various regional jets as well as the 70-seater Dash 8-400 and, despite its long association with Bombardier (builder of the Dash 8), the order for seven aircraft plus 14 options was for the Brazilian-built Embraer ERJ-145 already flown by British Regional. These will be delivered between 2000 and 2001, initially to be based at Bristol with other aircraft going to Manchester. The options may be varied to allow delivery of the smaller ERJ-135 which has already flown, or the larger ERJ-170 which is due to fly in 2001. Today Brymon operates services from bases at Aberdeen, Bristol, Manchester and Plymouth covering a substantial domestic network with destinations including Birmingham, Edinburgh, Newcastle, Glasgow and Newquay as well as both Jersey and Guernsey. International routes include Paris and Cork, and the acquisition of regional jets will allow expansion including new European services from Birmingham.

CityFlyer Express

CityFlyer is now a wholly owned subsidiary of British Airways but was originally formed in 1991 by management staff from the defunct Air Europe Express which was forced to cease operations when Air Europe collapsed. Initially the title Euroworld was adopted but in February 1992 the name was changed to CityFlyer Express. In April of that year the airline became the first British operator of the successful ATR42 turboprop airliner, and was also the first with the larger ATR72, in October 1994. Following on from a successful marketing agreement with British Airways, CityFlyer pioneered the British Airways franchise scheme when it became the first British Airways Express operator in August 1993, and its aircraft were subsequently repainted in BA livery. The early route network included domestic scheduled services from London Gatwick to Newcastle, Leeds, Jersey, Guernsey and international services to Antwerp, Dublin, Düsseldorf and Rotterdam; a Luton-Paris route was short-lived and abandoned after a few months. The last Shorts 360 was phased out of service at the end of 1995, following orders for further ATR72s. Routes to Amsterdam and Cologne/Bonn were started in 1996 and a substantial increase in traffic, partly due to the success of the BA Express franchise, led to an order for two Avro RJ100s in mid-1996 which entered service in March and April 1997. Subsequently, the airline has ordered several more Avro RJ100s so that nine aircraft will be in service by April 2000 while, at the same time, it has started to phase out some of the smaller ATR42s. By the summer of 1999 CityFlyer could boast a total of 706 flights a week to 15 destinations in the UK, Ireland, Holland, France, Germany, Switzerland, Luxembourg and the Channel Islands from its London Gatwick base. In addition, it operates winter and summer charter flights for a variety of tour companies including flights to Jersey and Guernsey from eight UK regional airports.

The partnership with British Airways proved so fruitful and successful that in November 1998 it was announced that British Airways would be purchasing a 100% shareholding in CityFlyer, making it a wholly owned subsidiary. This take-over was subject to government approval, which was given in late 1999 following an investigation by the Competition Commission on behalf of the Office of Fair Trading. It is intended that CityFlyer will retain its independent identity alongside British Airways at Gatwick but consideration is being given to obtaining larger aircraft such as the Boeing 737 or Airbus A319/320 to cater for further expansion, including some services currently flown by British Airways (European).

Go Fly Ltd

Faced with competition from low-cost operators such as Ryanair, EasyJet and Debonair, British Airways countered by setting up a new subsidiary under the brief but effective title Go. Headed by Barbara Cassani, an American with wide airline experience, and based at Stansted, the no-frills airline began operations on 22 May 1998 with an inaugural service to Rome but the network was quickly expanded to include Bologna, Copenhagen, Lisbon and Edinburgh. As more aircraft became available, services to Munich and Venice were added at the end of the year by which time the fleet had grown to seven Boeing 737-300s, and a service to Milan began the following year. These original aircraft had been previously operated by other airlines such as Philippine Airlines, Garuda and Air Liberté but the first of six brand-new Boeing 737-36N aircraft was delivered in October 1998 with the rest following in 1999 and the current fleet stands at 13 aircraft. Although wholly owned by British Airways, Go is run as a completely independent unit and does not necessarily rely on the parent airline for support services. For example, engineering support and aircraft maintenance is carried out by Stansted-based FLS Aerospace which won the contract in competition with British Airways' own engineering establishment.

Go is also unique as a British Airways subsidiary in that its livery and brand image appear completely different, again emphasising its independence. In fact, there is a subtle relationship between the Go and British Airways colour schemes in that both have a mainly white fuselage with the lower fuselage and engines painted in a contrasting colour: standard blue on British Airways aircraft but varying colours on the Go 737s. All Go aircraft carry the company name and logo across the rear fuselage and tailfin rather than the varied schemes of British Airways, but the individual aircraft then carry a unique slogan which includes the carrier's name. Examples include 'go now', 'away we go' and 'get set go'.

Air Liberté

After some extremely complex commercial deals and legal wrangles, British Airways now has a major presence in France in the form of Air Liberté. The story began in September 1992 when British Airways announced that it had taken a 49.5% share in TAT European Airlines for a reported £17.5 million. This carrier had originally been formed in 1968 and, at the time of the take-over, was France's second largest airline. The cash injection from British Airways allowed TAT to develop new routes which it had been awarded following a series of mergers between Air France and other airlines. In addition, British Airways was given the option of purchasing the remaining shareholding in 1997 and this was duly exercised, making TAT a wholly owned subsidiary. In the meantime, another French independent, Air Liberté, was in serious financial trouble and on the verge of bankruptcy. British Airways moved in and bought the airline in November 1996. There was little commercial sense in operating the two airlines as separate entities and they were duly merged under the Air Liberté title early in 1998. In fact, the route network of the two airlines was complementary, with the former TAT flying mostly domestic services using a fleet of ATR turboprops, Fokker F28s and Fokker 100s, and a few Boeing 737 jets, while Air Liberté had more international routes, particularly to Portugal and North Africa, as well as flying charter services using a fleet of MD-80s and DC-10s. Inevitably there will be some fleet rationalisation but for the moment all these types remain in service and they are gradually being repainted in the standard British Airways

Above: **British Airways' French operations started with a shareholding in TAT in 1992. Subsequently, this became a wholly-owned subsidiary which was merged with Air Liberté following the take-over of that airline in 1996. All aircraft in the fleet now carry the Air Liberté titles. Shown here is Fokker 100 F-GIOI which had previously flown in TAT colours.** *Author*

livery but with uniquely French world images on the tail. The group has filed some poor financial results to date, mainly due to the intense level of competition on French domestic routes as well as the extensive TGV rail network. However, British Airways is confident that it will make a commercial success of this venture and, in the meantime, it has established a very strong operational base within France.

Deutsche BA

At the end of World War 2 the victorious Allied powers allocated the rights to provide internal air services between Berlin and West Germany to British, US and French airlines. Although the latter soon dropped out, BEA (and, later, British Airways) together with Pan American continued to operate a comprehensive German route network until the German unification in the early 1990s rendered the arrangement out of date. For many years BA used a fleet of BAC111s based at Berlin but these were eventually replaced with quieter Boeing 737s and in the final years by ATPs belonging to the airline's Highland Division. However, British Airways was keen to maintain the valuable connections it had built up in the German market and was able to achieve this by purchasing a 49% shareholding in Delta Air Regionalflugverkehr, a regional airline based at Friedrichshafen and flying scheduled services with a fleet of Saab 340s. The remaining 51% was held by a consortium of German banks and the airline was renamed as Deutsche BA. Since then, British Airways has increased its holding, initially to 65% in July 1997, and to 100% when it bought out the remaining bank holdings in April 1998, making Deutsche BA a wholly owned subsidiary.

British Airways planned a substantial development programme for the new airline with new Boeing 737-300s, the first of these being delivered in June 1992 and the airline's first commercial jet service as Deutsche BA, from Berlin to Stuttgart and Munich, took place on the 29th of that month. Since then the jet fleet has expanded and now consists of a total of 21 Boeing 737-300s with more on order. Pending deliveries of some of the 737s, a fleet of five Fokker 100s were leased from BA's French subsidiary TAT from 1993 onwards but these were later returned as the 737 fleet built up, the last being released in January 1998. Deutsche BA originally incorporated a fleet of Saab 340 turboprop airliners which were gradually being replaced by the faster and larger Saab 2000, the first of which was delivered in March 1995. This remarkable aircraft had a cruising speed of 360kt and, among other routes, was used to operate a Gatwick to Bremen service, taking only 5min

longer than the Boeing 737 which it had replaced. However, in October 1996 it was announced that the airline was selling its turboprop operations, including both aircraft and access to the routes they served, to the Nantes-based Regional Airlines so that it could concentrate on building up its jet routes.

Deutsche BA's aircraft were originally painted in a colour scheme very similar to the then current British Airways pattern with a dark blue lower fuselage and pearl white upper surfaces. However, the tail fin was finished in a similar style to British Airways' aircraft but incorporated the German national colours of red, yellow and black, while a thin yellow and red cheat line ran down the fuselage. When the Utopia livery was adopted, Deutsche BA followed suit but its world image tail designs are specifically Germanic in origin. Deutsche BA's main route network covers internal German services linking Munich with Hamburg, Düsseldorf, Cologne and Berlin, and others from Berlin to Düsseldorf, Cologne and Stuttgart. International routes connect British Airways long-haul routes into Gatwick with Munich and Hamburg, while other destinations include Helsinki and Madrid.

British Airways Franchise Airlines

In 1993, further expansion of the British Airways brand was achieved by the introduction of a new concept in which other airlines, while still

Above: **Deutsche BA operates an all-Boeing 737 fleet which are finished in the basic British Airways colour scheme but with tail images having national connotations. This is D-ADBH which carries the Bavaria design.** *Mike Barth*

remaining independent, acted in co-operation under the British Airways Express title. The scheme was very successful and following City Flyer Express, the first franchisee, others such as Loganair and Manx European were quick to follow. Over the years the number of franchise airlines has steadily grown and many of them are based outside the UK. The term British Airways Express has since been dropped and all franchise operators share the common British Airways image.

BASE Airlines

This Dutch airline became the 10th British Airways franchise company, early in 1999. It currently flies to Birmingham, Gatwick, Manchester and Zurich from Rotterdam and Eindhoven, the latter being its own operating base. The fleet currently consists of three 16-seat Jetstream 31s and two 28-seat Embraer EMB-120 Brasilias. However, it is actively considering the acquisition of 50-seater regional jets and will go ahead with this if business increases as anticipated.

British Mediterranean Airways

This airline started operations under the chairmanship of Lord Hesketh in October 1994 with a five-times-a-week service from London to Beirut using a single Airbus A320. Expansion of services to other Mediterranean and Middle East destinations including Amman and Damascus occurred in 1995 and subsequently there was a certain amount of duplication of effort between British Mediterranean and British Airways. In 1996 it was announced that the former would

become a British Airways franchise airline and that British Airways would withdraw its own services from Beirut, Amman and Damascus. For various technical and administrative reasons, this was not implemented, as originally planned, for the 1996-7 winter season but was delayed until the beginning of the summer 1997 timetable. In order to meet its new commitments, British Mediterranean has expanded its fleet to a total of three Airbus A320s by leasing two ex-China Airways aircraft. In addition to the services already listed, the airline commenced flights to Tbilisi in Georgia and Alexandria in Egypt during April 1997. Other destinations now served include Yerevan (Armenia) and Ashgabat (Turkmenistan).

British Regional Airlines

This was the title adopted by Manx Airlines (Europe) as from September 1996. Aircraft were finished in British Airways Express livery and carried the British Regional Airlines title on the nose. The change of name was partly implemented in order to provide a separate corporate image and avoid confusion with sister

Below: **British Mediterranean Airlines became a franchise operator in 1997. It currently flies three Airbus A320s powered by V2500 turbofans, in contrast to British Airways' own aircraft which are CFM56-powered. A fourth aircraft was on order at the end of 1999 to cater for expanded services to Amman and Damascus.** *British Mediterranean Airlines/Adrian Meredith*

company Manx Airlines which continued to operate independently under its own colours from its Ronaldsway base, and both companies were in turn subsidiaries of the British Regional Airlines Group. This latter organisation was originally part of the Airlines of Britain Group, closely linked with British Midland, but all ties with this great rival to British Airways were severed in 1998. At its inception, the British Regional fleet comprised a single BAe146 (the first example to be seen in British Airways colours), nine BAe ATPs, 12 Jetstream 41s and two Jetstream 31s. In October 1996 the Scottish BA Express operator, Loganair, was absorbed into British Regional Airlines which then became responsible for the operation of all British Airways internal Scottish services. However, this arrangement did not last long and Loganair again became an independent operator, although still a BA franchisee, in early 1997. Having got over its birth pangs, British Regional expanded rapidly and today has major hubs at several British airports including Aberdeen, Edinburgh, Southampton, Cardiff and Manchester. Its summer route network covers almost 50 destinations and although most of these are domestic routes, it also serves points such as Paris, Zurich, Hanover, Dublin and Shannon. In March 1999 it announced plans to begin a substantial range of services from the new Sheffield City airport which had opened the previous year. On the equipment side, British Regional was the first UK airline to order the Embraer ERJ-145 50-seater regional jet and a total of 15 were due to be in service by March 2000, with another five for delivery by September 2002. Options are also held on five additional aircraft. In due course these will gradually replace the turboprops in the British Regional fleet and enable the airline to develop further domestic and European routes. Already, apart from its own services, British Regional also leases some ERJs to British Airways to provide additional frequency on key routes out of Manchester.

Comair

Nothing could better illustrate the worldwide aspirations of British Airways than its recruitment of the South African airline Comair

to the franchise fold in 1996. Passengers using British Airways long-haul flights to South Africa from London can now benefit from Comair's extensive domestic network which includes Cape Town, Durban and Johannesburg, as well as international connections to Harare (Zimbabwe) and Windhoek (Namibia). The original fleet which included a mixture of jets and turboprops has been rationalised and now comprises four Boeing 727s (the only examples of the type ever to wear British Airways livery) and six Boeing 737-200s, including two ex-British Airways aircraft. Comair was originally formed in 1946 and is now the largest privately owned airline in South Africa. It operates 250 flights a week and holds 35% of the domestic passenger market.

GB Airways

This airline was originally formed as Gibraltar Airways in 1930 as a subsidiary of the Bland shipping company and was based on the rock after which it was named. Services ceased in 1932 and the company lay dormant until 1947 when BEA took over a 51% shareholding and adopted the name Gibair. In this form the airline flew services from Gibraltar to the UK and also to North Africa. When BEA was absorbed into British Airways, the Gibair shareholding was reduced to 49% but services continued as before. The title GB Airways was adopted in 1980 and since then traffic has increased considerably, necessitating the introduction of jets. In 1994 all services to North Africa were transferred to Heathrow, while Gibraltar and Madeira were served from Gatwick. GB Airways became a BA Express operator in 1995 and the aircraft, including a pair of modern 737-400s leased from British Airways, adopted BA livery. Subsequently, the older 737-200s were phased out and the current fleet comprises four 737-300s, including two ordered directly from Boeing, and five 737-400s. Following on from British Airways' large order for Airbus narrow bodies, GB Airways has placed orders for nine aircraft which will be a mix of 159-seater A320s and 198-seater A321s. These will be delivered between 2001 and 2003. GB Airways now plays an important role alongside the British Airways European operation at Gatwick and currently serves some 16 destinations in Spain, Portugal,

Tunisia and Morocco, as well as Gibraltar and Malta. In addition it also flies to Alicante, Malaga and Faro from Heathrow.

Loganair

Loganair is one of the oldest existing British Airlines and has had rather a chequered history, particularly in recent years. It was formed in 1962 and became part of the Airlines of Britain group (ABG) in December 1983. Early services concentrated on routes from Glasgow and Edinburgh to the Scottish Highlands and Islands and, since 1973, it has been responsible for the Scottish Air Ambulance service. In the 1980s the airline considerably expanded its route network and flew several UK domestic routes including the Channel Islands and Manchester. However, a reorganisation in 1994 led to many services — and its fleet of ATPs and Bae146s — being transferred to Manx Airlines (Europe) while Loganair became a British Airways Express operator, although still part of the ABG. The remaining fleet consisted of five Islanders and eight Shorts 360s which were painted in BA Express colours and operated an extensive network of services around Scotland, including the socially important Highlands and Islands routes. In October 1996 Loganair was absorbed into the newly formed British Regional Airlines and lost its separate identity. However, this arrangement was short-lived and Loganair re-emerged as an independent operator in March 1997 following a management buyout, although it remained a British Airways franchisee and the aircraft retained BA liveries. At this stage the fleet consisted of five Islanders, a Twin Otter and five Shorts 360s, but two Saab 340s were added in mid-1999 to replace some of the elderly unpressurised Shorts 360s on longer sectors. The Islanders continue to operate the Scottish Air Ambulance service and the airline's route network is almost entirely within Scotland, the main exception being a Glasgow to Londonderry service.

Maersk Air UK

Maersk Air UK was formed in 1993 to take over the former assets of Birmingham European Airlines (BEA) which had been merged in 1992 with Brymon Airways to form Brymon European. When this airline was demerged in 1993,

Maersk Air (a Danish airline) took over 100% shareholding in the former BEA in which it had previously been only a 40% shareholder. After being painted briefly in Maersk colours, the aircraft were repainted yet again in 1994 when Maersk Air UK became a BA franchise operator. Apart from a Birmingham-Newcastle service operated by a turboprop Jetstream, the rest of the route network consisted of international flights to European destinations initially flown by a fleet of six ex-British Airways BAC111s which, no doubt, were surprised to find themselves back in their former owner's livery! Pending the introduction of five modern Boeing 737-500s leased from the parent Maersk, the long-lived BAC111s were replaced with some of the British Airways 737-200 fleet but these have also now been retired. Maersk's most significant move was to order the Bombardier CRJ-200LR Regional Jet, the first British airline to do so, and deliveries began in the summer of 1998 with a total of eight due in service by April 2000. Orders for three of the larger 70-seater CRJ-700 (plus three options) were announced in late 1999 with deliveries due from 2001 onwards. Currently, Maersk Air operates almost 300 services a week from its Birmingham hub to destinations including Amsterdam, Berlin, Copenhagen, Geneva, Lyon, Milan, Stuttgart, Venice, Belfast and Newcastle. Maersk Air's franchise agreement with British Airways expires in 2001 and, if not renewed, many of its routes will be taken over by BA Regional or Brymon.

National Jets Italia

This is the latest British Airways franchise operation and was set up in 1999 in order to gain access to the Italian passenger market which, until recently, has been mostly monopolised by the state carrier, Alitalia. Initially using a fleet of five British Aerospace 146-300s painted in British Airways colours with the Union Flag tail image, flights from Rome to Palermo and Catania were due to start in early 2000 while services from Turin, Milan and Florence to London were expected to follow. The aircraft will be flown and operated by National Jet Systems which has links with British World Airlines. British Airways has high hopes for the success of this operation, having stated that it considers

Above: **The Scottish regional airline Loganair has been a British Airways franchisee since 1994. In that time it has undergone a number of changes of management but retains the BA associations. It currently operates a mixed fleet of Islanders and Shorts 360s, although some of the latter are being replaced by the faster Saab 340, two of which are currently in service. Shown here is Shorts 360 G-BPFN, appropriately sporting the Benyhone Tartan image.** *Author*

the Italian market to have the highest growth potential of any in Europe.

Sun Air of Scandinavia

Early in 1996 Sun Air of Scandinavia became the first non-UK independent to adopt the British Airways franchise. At the time it flew a fleet of Jetstream 31s and 41s on commuter services throughout Denmark and southern Scandinavia, centred mainly on Copenhagen although the airline's headquarters was at Billund in the west of Denmark. Sun Air was formed in 1977 and also operates a fleet of executive jets and turboprops for charter work in addition to its scheduled service network. Sun Air plays an important role by providing feeder passengers to British Airways' extensive route network from Manchester and as a result of healthy load factors it ordered British Aerospace ATPs for delivery in September 1997 to replace the Jetstream 41s currently used on this route. The Jetstream 31 fleet will be reduced and jet equipment may be introduced around the year 2000.

oneworld™

The widespread use of computer-based airline reservation systems has allowed the principle of code-sharing to become widely established. Under this scheme airlines can co-operate on

various routes and operate services on behalf of each other. These flights are listed by both the airlines concerned using their own flight numbers but will only be operated by one of the partners. The fare-paying passenger is often surprised to find that having bought a ticket from one carrier, he or she is being flown by another. This scheme can have great benefits for the airlines concerned, bringing in extra passengers and avoiding wasteful duplication of flights. In recent years this system has been taken a stage further with several airlines sharing codes and other benefits in order to build up a worldwide network of allied airlines. In response to this trend, British Airways was instrumental in setting up a new grouping in February 1999 under the title **one**world™. Claimed to be the world's largest airline alliance grouping, **one**world™ offers passengers some substantial benefits including global fares, reciprocal rewards programmes, common lounge access and a greatly enhanced choice of routes and timings. Details of the **one**world™ airline partners are listed below.

American Airlines

This airline, the second largest in the US, was in discussion with British Airways from 1996 over a proposal to form a close operating alliance which would have given the two airlines a 20% share of the lucrative transatlantic traffic

Above: **American Airlines is a significant British Airways ally and there is a strong business relationship between these two major airlines. American was one of the founders of the one**world™ **partnership.** *Author*

Below: **Birmingham-based Maersk Air UK is the only British airline to operate the Bombardier CRJ Regional Jet (pictured here). It also flies five Boeing 737-500s.** *Bombardier Aerospace*

Bottom: **The Australian flag carrier QANTAS has had a long association with British Airways for many years before becoming a one**world™ **partner.** *Author*

as well as building up a powerful worldwide route network. Political and commercial opposition effectively delayed and prevented a formal merger but the co-operation resulting from the talks formed the basis of the current **one**world™ alliance.

American Airlines' history can be traced back as far as 1930 when a number of airlines merged to form American Airways, the name being changed to its present form in 1934. It grew rapidly in the prewar period and after 1945 resumed full commercial operations including its first transatlantic services through a subsidiary known as American Overseas Airlines. It began operating jets, Boeing 707s, in January 1959 and a decade later was an early customer for the Boeing 747 and the driving force behind the launch of the DC-10. Its current substantial presence at London Heathrow dates from the early 1990s when it took over TWA's transatlantic services. American Airlines' fleet currently numbers over 600 aircraft including 35 Airbus A300s, 11 Boeing MD-11s and over 70 Boeing 767s for long-haul services although, unusually for a major airline, it does not operate the Boeing 747. The rest of the fleet includes Boeing 727s, 737s and 757s, as well as MD-80s and Fokker 100s, these being used mostly on the extensive US domestic network.

Canadian Airlines (International)

Until recently Canadian Airlines was one of two major Canadian carriers (the other was Air Canada) and had various marketing agreements and code-sharing arrangements in place for some time before formally joining the **one**world™ alliance. Its history can be traced back to 1942 when the railroad company, Canadian Pacific, formed an airline of the same name. In the postwar years this grew rapidly and began international services in 1949 using DC-4s to pioneer a route across the Pacific from Vancouver to Sydney. Services to Amsterdam, Tokyo and Hong Kong with turboprop Britannias started in 1958 and Canadian Pacific joined the jet age in 1961, ordering a fleet of DC-8s which eventually replaced the Britannia and the piston-engined fleet. During the 1980s it took over a number of Canadian regional carriers and this process culminated with a merger with Pacific Western

Airlines. The resulting company was renamed Canadian Airlines, with its headquarters at Calgary, and the long-haul charter airline Wardair was taken over the following year. The current fleet includes some 25 long-haul aircraft (Boeing 747, 767, DC-10) as well as approximately 40 Boeing 737s and Airbus A320s, and these are operated as Canadian Airlines International. Canadian Airlines also owns Canadian Regional Airlines which is responsible for the domestic network flown by the various regional carriers acquired by the parent company. Together these operate a fleet of around 650 turboprops throughout Canada and parts of North America. The two elements of Canadian Airlines are an important link in the **one**world™ global route network but their future is in some doubt as Canadian Airlines was taken over by a group led by Air Canada in late 1999. At the moment, Canadian continues as a separate subsidiary but, as Air Canada is a major player in the rival Star group, the **one**world™ commitment may be in jeopardy.

QANTAS

The Australian national flag carrier can trace its history back to 1920 and the formation of the Queensland and Northern Territory Aerial Service (QANTAS). After World War 2 the airline was nationalised in 1947 and developed an extensive worldwide network. It was the first airline outside the United States to operate the Boeing 707 (in 1959) and was an early customer for the Boeing 747. Its current fleet consists of 30 Boeing 767-200s and -300ERs and around 30 Boeing 747s, including 21 of the latest 400 series which are replacing some of the older 200 series aircraft. While QANTAS mainly operated international services, domestic flights were operated by a number of airlines including Australian Airlines. Prior to the privatisation of QANTAS in 1995, the airline took a 100% holding in Australian Airlines which maintained a comprehensive domestic network with a fleet of 38 Boeing 737-300s and -400s, and subsequently the two airlines were merged. In 1992, in preparation for the deregulation of Australian air services and the privatisation of both QANTAS and Australian Airlines, the Australian government invited bidders for a 25% stake in QANTAS and the British Airways offer of £296 million was accepted at the end of 1992. This shareholding gave the British airline a welcome access to the Australian market as well as strengthening links in the important Southeast Asia and Pacific regions and BA will have the opportunity to bid for a further share in the future. There is also a degree of fleet commonality as QANTAS' 747-400s are the same Rolls-Royce-powered versions used by British Airways. Since 1995 the two airlines have rationalised their schedules on the so called 'Kangaroo Route' between the UK and Australia with mutual advantages to both organisations.

QANTAS also operates extensive regional services throughout Australia by means of wholly owned subsidiaries Airlink, Eastern Australia Airlines, Southern Australia Airlines and Sunstate Airlines. These operate a variety of commuter and regional airliners including the BAe146 and Jetstream, DHC Dash 8s, and Shorts 330/360s. These aircraft are all painted in QANTAS' livery.

Cathay Pacific

A Hong Kong-based airline originally formed in 1946 with a couple of ex-military DC-3s. In the 1950s it expanded considerably using DC-4s and DC-6s to fly longer routes throughout Southeast Asia. Its first jets, Convair CV880s, were ordered in 1960 and from that time it grew rapidly on the back of the boom economy of Hong Kong. Like most long-haul airlines, it invested heavily in the new wide-bodied jets in the 1970s and flew both Boeing 747s and TriStars although the latter were phased out as deliveries of new Airbus A330s and 340s began in 1995. The current fleet is exclusively long-haul and totals over 70 aircraft including new Boeing 777s as well as the 747s and the Airbus 330/340s. Cathay Pacific retains a 25% shareholding in the regional carrier Dragonair and a 75% stake in Air Hong Kong, a dedicated cargo airline operating with two Boeing 747 freighters. With an extensive route network connecting all major points in Southeast Asia and Australasia with Europe and the United States, Cathay is a very important member of the **one**world™ alliance.

Iberia

The Spanish national flag carrier can trace its origins back to 1927 and currently flies to almost 100 destinations in 44 countries. It is particularly strong in former Spanish colonial areas such as South and Central America. Its substantial fleet of over 100 aircraft includes the Airbus A300, A320, A340, Boeing 727, 737, 747, 757 and 767 as well as the MD-87 and Douglas DC-10. It has been state-owned since

Above: **Aer Lingus is the latest airline to join oneworld™, in December 1999. British Airways is also negotiating to purchase a shareholding when the state-owned airline is privatised.** *Author*

the Spanish government took a controlling share in 1938 but more recently there have been moves to privatise the airline. Currently the government share has been reduced to 54% while various investors hold the rest. These include British Airways, which has a 9% stake in a joint agreement with American Airlines, which has taken a nominal 1% share, to give the two partners a 10% holding. Iberia became a member of the **one**world™ alliance in September 1999 and further co-operation and rationalisation of services can be expected.

Finnair

The Finnish national airline formally joined the **one**world™ alliance in September 1999 but had previously concluded an operating agreement with British Airways at the beginning of 1998. Finnair is one of the world's oldest airlines, tracing a continuous history back to 1923, although services were halted during World War 2. The airline's long-haul fleet consists of four MD-11s, but it maintains a comprehensive network of regional services throughout Scandinavia and Europe, including many Russian destinations. These are flown by a mixture of MD-80 series twinjets, Boeing 757s and turboprop ATR 72s and Saab 340s. Deliveries of a substantial order for the Airbus A320 family of aircraft commenced early in 1999.

Aer Lingus

The Irish state airline officially joined the **one**world™ alliance on 2 December 1999. The Irish government also intends to privatise the airline and when this occurs the British Airways/American Airlines combination has expressed an interest in taking a 10% shareholding. Originally formed in 1936, Aer Lingus' development was virtually halted by World War 2 but scheduled services recommenced in 1945 and gradually expanded to cover a network within the British Isles and later into Europe. Transatlantic services began in 1958 using leased Lockheed Constellations until the first Boeing 707 jets were acquired in 1960. Aer Lingus was an early customer for the Fokker Friendship turboprop and also operated Viscounts and Shorts 360s as well as BAC111s and Boeing 737s. The current fleet includes Airbus A321s and Boeing 737-400/-500s for European routes and Airbus A330 for long-haul services. Aer Lingus Commuter is a wholly owned subsidiary which operates BAe146s and Fokker 50s mostly on the busy routes between Ireland and the UK mainland. These latter services will provide significant feeder traffic to **one**world™ partners' long-haul routes.

LAN Chile

This South American airline is expected to become a member of the **one**world™ team in 2000. It was originally formed as a private airline in 1929 but was nationalised and given its present title in 1932. Like many airlines in the region it has had a chequered history but was eventually privatised again in 1989 since when it has become one of the major airlines in South America. Its current route network is mostly within South America, with other services to Mexico and the United Sates. Its sole European destination is Frankfurt. Most regional services are flown by Boeing 737s but these are due to be replaced by some 20 Airbus A319s and A320s over the next few years. Long-haul routes are flown by a fleet of 12 Boeing 767-300ERs.

British Airways and its **one**world™ partners are constantly looking for other airlines to join the alliance. At the time of writing Japan Airlines has negotiated a code-sharing agreement with British Airways on some routes and it is expected to join the **one**world™ alliance during 2000.

Finally, British Airways currently has code-sharing agreements with America West, Malev and LOT Polish Airlines and owns a small shareholding in Air Mauritius. Taken together with the list of subsidiaries, partners and franchise operations outlined in the foregoing, it can be seen that there is no corner of the world which is not served by British Airways or its associates in one form or another. Truly a global operation!

3. Aircraft

Modern airliners are much more efficient than their predecessors of even a decade ago. Embodying the latest advances in aerodynamics, engine technology, computerised avionics and flight management systems, the new products from the major manufacturers offer the capability of generating substantial incomes for the airlines that can operate them efficiently. Although expensive to buy, large airliners such as the Boeing 777 can be expected to remain in service for around 25 years, perhaps even longer. British Airways, therefore, needs to be sure that it has selected the right aircraft when it places substantial orders to replace and modernise its fleet of several hundred aircraft. Although there is plenty of choice when choosing smaller airliners carrying 100 passengers or less, there are now only two western airframe manufacturers building the larger aircraft which form the major part of the British Airways fleet — Airbus and Boeing. When the airline was first formed in 1974, its fleet was made up of a diverse variety of types inherited from its predecessors, BOAC and BEA, and while the long-haul fleet virtually standardised on the Boeing 747 as the older Boeing 707s and Vickers VC10s were retired, it was another decade before substantial numbers of Boeing 737s and 757s began to replace types such as the Hawker Siddeley Trident and BAC111 in the medium and short-haul fleets. Another significant aircraft was the graceful Lockheed TriStar, initially inherited from a BEA order, and the take-over of British Caledonian in 1988 led to new types in the shape of McDonnell Douglas DC-10s and Airbus A320s also being absorbed into the fleet. Despite these exceptions, British Airways stayed a staunch Boeing customer, placing repeat orders for 747s, 757s and 737s, as well as the subsequent Boeing 767 and, more recently, the Boeing 777.

However, a review of the airline's corporate strategy in 1999 has led to a change of emphasis which will significantly alter the size and composition of the fleet in the new millennium. In an effort to combat what is seen as global overcapacity, British Airways is now aiming specifically at business and other high-yield passengers and will carry relatively fewer low-yield economy class passengers. This translates to a requirement for smaller aircraft on many routes so that, for example, new orders for Boeing 747-400s are being cancelled in favour of the twin-engined Boeing 777. Some Boeing 767s will be retired, as will most of the Boeing 757 fleet. The latter will be replaced by the smaller Airbus A320 (and possibly the A321) while A319s and A318s will provide the solution to the long-standing requirement to replace the old Boeing 737-200s operated by British Airways Regional at Manchester and Birmingham. The order for up to 188 Airbus aircraft, announced in 1998, represented a major success for the European consortium and was won despite strong competition from Boeing.

The rationalisation of the fleet has been helped by the transfer of many domestic and European routes to subsidiary and franchise airlines so that small regional jets and turboprop airliners are no longer part of the mainline fleet. In the three years since the last edition of this book was published, British Airways has retired all of its DC-10s and the British Aerospace ATP is no longer flown by the parent company, although it is still used by some franchise operators. In addition, all of the early series Boeing 747-146s have been retired, as have a substantial number of the Boeing 737-236s, leaving only a few with the Regional Divisions awaiting replacement by the new Airbus aircraft. However, some things never change and the supersonic Concorde is still the glamorous flagship of the fleet despite having been originally ordered by BOAC in the 1960s.

Aircraft of the British Airways Mainline, European and Regional Fleets

The following pages present a review and specification of each of the aircraft types currently operated by (or on order for) the British Airways Mainline, European and Regional fleets. These are:

- Aérospatiale/British Aerospace Concorde
- Boeing 737-200
- Boeing 747 Classic
- Boeing 757
- Airbus A318/319/320
- Boeing 737-300/-400
- Boeing 747-400
- Boeing 767
- Boeing 777

Aircraft owned and operated by British Airways' subsidiaries and franchise operators are briefly described in a separate listing.

Aérospatiale/British Aerospace Concorde

Technical Data
Dimensions and Weights

Length:	203ft 9in	Max Take-off Weight:	408,000lb (185,070kg)
Span:	83ft 8in	Operating Empty Weight:	189,400lb (85,900kg)
Height:	37ft 1in	Max Fuel:	94,750kg
Wing Area:	3,856sq ft (358.25sq m)		

Powerplants
Four Rolls-Royce/Snecma Olympus 593 turbojets. Each 38,050lb thrust with reheat.

Performance and Payload

Max Cruising Speed:	1,176kt (Mach 2.0)
Economic Cruising Speed:	-
Range (Max Fuel):	3,550nm
Range (Max Payload):	3,360nm
Passenger Capacity:	100
Cargo Capacity:	1,300lb (590kg)

Concorde is absolutely unique and provides British Airways with a high-profile flagship for its prestigious transatlantic services which no other airline, apart from Air France, can match. Taking just over 3hr for the 3,000-mile crossing to New York or 4hr to Washington, the graceful supersonic airliner flies well above the slower conventional jets at altitudes up to 60,000ft while its passengers relax in sumptuous comfort, pampered by British Airways' renowned service. Concorde is something special!

It is therefore all the more sobering to realise that the prototype first flew as long ago as 2 March 1969, although an exhaustive 5,000hr test programme to investigate thoroughly the untried concept of safe commercial supersonic flight delayed the inauguration of scheduled services by British Airways until January 1976. Changing circumstances in the intervening years caused a dramatic downturn in

Concorde's fortunes and airlines which had flocked to place options for up to 74 aircraft gradually fell by the wayside in the face of rising fuel prices and growing environmental pressures. It was not until June 1972 that British Airways placed a firm order for five Concordes, and these were all delivered in the course of 1976/7. Due to action by US environmental groups, Concorde was initially not permitted to operate into American airports and consequently the first supersonic schedules were to Bahrain. However, services to Washington started in May 1976 and to New York in the following November. Subsequently, British Airways entered into agreements with other airlines in an attempt to broaden Concorde's route structure. At the end of 1977 a joint service to Singapore via Bahrain was inaugurated in conjunction with Singapore Airlines but this was abandoned after a few flights due to problems connected with

Left: **Despite its unrivalled performance, Concorde is still very much 1960s technology. The flightdeck is crammed with analogue instruments in contrast to the electronic displays now seen in all modern aircraft.**
Ian James

overflying Malaysia. Eventually, the service was restarted and ran for almost two years from January 1979 but as much of the flight was overland, there were few opportunities for supersonic flight. In 1979 a leasing agreement with Braniff resulted in the Washington service being extended to Dallas/Fort Worth but this lasted only until May 1980.

In 1980, under an agreement reached with the government, who decided to write off all Concorde development costs so that the aircraft could operate on a purely commercial basis, British Airways took delivery of two further aircraft and in 1982 set up a new Concorde Division which today is entirely responsible for all aspects of the aircraft, including its commercial profitability. Scheduled services are now concentrated on the all-important transatlantic routes to New York and Washington, and in winter direct flights to Barbados are flown at weekends. In addition, the aircraft has been available for charter and some spectacular flights have been made, breaking numerous records in the process. Despite a few well-publicised incidents, Concorde has an excellent safety record which bears comparison with any conventional subsonic airliner and has already carried well over one million passengers. The interior of the cabin is split into two compartments, of 40 and 60 seats respectively, by a central bulkhead and is sumptuously fitted out, with the 100 passengers reclining in luxurious seats upholstered in grey leather. The whole Concorde fleet was refurbished and fitted with new galleys, improved cabin lighting, and a new high-quality audio entertainment system, in 1993-4. A further modernisation and upgrade

has been carried out more recently in order to maintain the high standards expected by the premium passengers flying in this aircraft.

Following on from the two development prototypes (001 and 002), two pre-production (01 and 02) and 14 production aircraft were built. The prototypes are now both in museums while the pre-production aircraft are stored by the manufacturers, leaving the remainder evenly split between British Airways and Air France. At the end of the 20th century the aircraft had been in service for well over 20 years but a British Airways-led engineering programme has increased the permitted number of flight cycles from 6,700 to 8,500 for each aircraft and this should allow Concorde operations to continue up to 2014 when the last aircraft will finally be retired. However, Concorde has shown that there is a market for high-speed travel at premium fares and all the major airframe manufacturers, including British Aerospace, have looked at a possible 250-seater successor. Whether such an aircraft will ever be built remains open to speculation. A more intriguing alternative is beginning to emerge from the various studies for supersonic business jets. These appear much more likely to be built and could be developed into a small 20-seater airliner in the same way that the first of the current regional jets evolved from subsonic business jets. Small supersonic airliners would allow many airlines to get into a market niche so far dominated by Concorde, still regarded by many as the most beautiful aircraft ever built.

Unlike many other aircraft in the British Airways fleet, Concordes do not carry individual names.

Airbus A320 and Derivatives

Technical Data: Airbus A320
Dimensions and Weights

Length:	123ft 3in (37.57m)	Max Take-off Weight:	158,700lb (72,000kg)
Span:	111ft 3in (33.91m)	Operating Empty Weight:	85,000lb (38,900kg)
Height:	38ft 7in (11.76m)	Max Fuel:	19,159kg
Wing Area:	1,318sq ft (122.4sq m)		

Powerplants
Two CFM International CFM56-5 turbofans. Each 25,000lb thrust.

Performance and Payload

Max Cruising Speed:	487kt at 28,000ft
Economic Cruising Speed:	454kt at 37,000ft
Range (Max Fuel):	3,750nm
Range (Max Payload):	2,300nm
Passenger Capacity:	Up to 149 passengers
Cargo Capacity:	1.8 tonnes (100 series), 2.3 tonnes (200 series)

Technical Data: Airbus A319
Dimensions and Weights

Length:	111ft 0in (33.84m)	Max Take-off Weight:	142,000lb (64,400kg)
Span:	111ft 10in (34.09m)	Operating Empty Weight:	88,400lb (40,100kg)
Height:	38ft 7in (11.76m)	Max Fuel:	19,184kg
Wing Area:	1,320sq ft (122.6sq m)		

Powerplants
Two International Aero Engine V2524 or V2527 turbofans; 23,480lb or 24,990lb thrust.

Performance and Payload

Max Cruising Speed:	Mach 0.82
Economic Cruising Speed:	446kt at 39,000ft
Range (Max Fuel):	4,710nm
Range (Max Payload):	2,455nm
Passenger Capacity:	Up to 124 passengers (mixed class)
Cargo Capacity:	Four LD3 containers

Technical Data: Airbus A318
Dimensions and Weights

Length:	103ft (31.44m)	Max Take-off Weight:	130,071lb (59,000kg)
Span:	111ft 3in (33.91m)	Operating Empty Weight:	86,046lb (39,030kg)
Height:	38ft 7in (11.76m)	Max Fuel:	19,184kg
Wing Area:	1,320sq ft (122.6sq m)		

Powerplants
Two Pratt & Whitney PW6000 turbofans. Each 23,990lb thrust.

Performance and Payload

Max Cruising Speed:	Mach 0.82
Economic Cruising Speed:	Mach 0.78
Range (Max Fuel):	3,760nm
Range (Max Payload):	1,540nm
Passenger Capacity:	Up to 107 passengers (mixed class)
Cargo Capacity:	none available

For over a decade the A320 has been the only Airbus product in the British Airways fleet and this occurred only as a result of the take-over of British Caledonian who, as one of the launch customers, had placed an order for 10 aircraft. The first of these, G-BUSB, had already been rolled out in BCAL colours and was hastily repainted in British Airways livery before delivery in March 1988. Another three aircraft had been delivered by the end of the year and a further three followed in 1989, with the remainder in 1990. The first five were actually Series 100 models, the others being the higher gross weight Series 200. Initially based at Gatwick, A320 operations were transferred to Heathrow in October 1988 and they are currently used on short and medium-range services to a variety of European destinations, but may also be seen on UK domestic routes. The aircraft are configured in a one-class 146-seat layout although the cabin can be divided by temporary partitions to allow use of a Club Class section when required on the European sectors.

Although well received by passengers, the most significant feature of the aircraft is the flightdeck with its distinctive sidesticks instead of conventional control columns, pointing to the fact that this aircraft employs a computer-driven Fly-By-Wire control system. When the pilot applies pressure to the sidestick (which actually moves only very slightly) the flight control system computers ensure that the control response is such that the aircraft will always remain in a safe operating envelope. Thus, for example, if the pilot were to attempt to overbank in a turn at low speed, a conventional aircraft would stall and possibly enter a spin whereas the A320 would automatically limit the angle of bank and, if necessary, automatically increase the engine thrust to maintain a safe flying attitude. All flight instrumentation, navigational information and systems status is shown on six interchangeable electronic display screens and the aircraft's sophisticated flight management system takes care of almost all the routine tasks associated with a flight.

Although the A320 was a technical success and liked by pilots and passengers alike, British Airways remained a firm Boeing customer for several major orders despite intense marketing efforts by the European consortium. However, in early 1996 British Airways announced a requirement for a substantial fleet of regional jets in the 120-160-seat class to replace the older 737s and the turboprop ATPs. In addition, it was expected that further aircraft would be ordered by subsidiary and franchise airlines. The ensuing sales battle for this substantial order was fought between Boeing, which offered the New Generation variants of the best selling 737, and Airbus with its rival family of jets based on the A320. In view of the British carrier's history of buying Boeing products, it was therefore a great coup for Airbus when the decision went in its favour. The size of the order announced in August 1998 was also a surprise to many observers, with no less than 59 firm orders and options for up to 129 additional aircraft. Of those on firm order, 20 were

Above: **British Airways World Cargo operates only one Boeing 747 Freighter in its own livery. This particular aircraft (N495MC) is leased from the US operator Atlas Air.** *J.Dibbs via British Airways*

Below left: **Despite intense competition from Boeing with its new 717, Airbus was again successful in gaining a further order for new aircraft to equip the British Airways Regional fleet. The Airbus family includes the A319 seen here and the A318 — the smallest derivative of the A320. The first aircraft in BA colours was delivered in October 1999.** *Airbus Industrie*

Below: **Visible evidence of the shattering power of Concorde's four Olympus turbojets is shown by the trailing heat haze on departure from Cardiff Wales airport.** *Malcolm Bradbury*

additional A320s, but the remainder were for the smaller A319 and the first of these entered service with British Airways Regional at Birmingham in October 1999. By May 2000 it is planned for there to be nine A319s based at Birmingham and later in the year further aircraft will be based at Manchester. Delivery of the first new A320s to British Airways will commence in 2002, these going to the European operation at Gatwick, although franchise operator GB Airways has also ordered nine A320s and these will be the first to see service, in 2000. Despite the fact that the original ex-BCAL A320s were powered by CFM56 turbofans, the new A320s and A319s will have International Aero Engines V2500 powerplants.

One of the main attractions of the Airbus family was the flexibility within the range of aircraft on offer. In a two-class seating configuration these varied from the 107-seater A318 to the 185-seater A321, all basically the same aircraft and allowing common pilot-type ratings and reduced engineering and

maintenance costs. To date, British Airways has not confirmed any orders for the larger A321 and initially deferred a decision at the lower end of the seating capacity in order to consider other types, notably the Boeing 717 which was keenly marketed by the manufacturer. However, the airline again went for the Airbus product and selected the A318, which is now scheduled to enter service with BA Regional in 2003. These will be powered by Pratt & Whitney PW6000 turbofans.

As related elsewhere, British Airways intends to begin disposing of most of its Boeing 757s and these will be replaced at Heathrow by a mix of 49 A319s and A320s which will join the existing 10 A320s already based there. Worldwide, over 2,000 of the Airbus A320 family have been ordered since the prototype first flew in 1987.

The original ex-BCAL A320s are named after British offshore islands but a naming policy for the newly ordered aircraft has not been announced.

Boeing 737-200

Technical Data
Dimensions and Weights

Length:	100ft (30.5m)	Max Take-off Weight:	116,300lb (52,750kg)
Span:	93ft (28.4m)	Operating Empty Weight:	61,000lb (27,670kg)
Height:	37ft (11.3m)	Max Fuel:	15,628kg
Wing Area:	980sq ft (91.04sq m)		

Powerplants
Two Pratt & Whitney JT8D-15A turbojets; 15,500lb thrust.

Performance and Payload

Max Cruising Speed:	500kt at 22,500ft
Economic Cruising Speed:	430kt at 30,000ft
Range (Max Fuel):	2,000nm
Range (Max Payload):	1,680nm
Passenger Capacity:	92/114
Cargo Capacity:	2.4 tonnes

The Boeing 737 lays claim to being the most successful airliner ever built and over 4,300 of all variants had been ordered by September 1999. The original 737-100 first flew in 1967, sometime after its contemporary rivals, the DC-9 and BAC111. Whereas the other aircraft opted for tail-mounted engines, the 737 retained the traditional wing-mounted configuration

mated to a fuselage with the same cross-section as the earlier 707 and 727 which allowed a generous six-abreast seating arrangement. The 737-100 was replaced by the 737-200 after only 30 of the former had been built, the new version featuring a 6ft fuselage stretch to accommodate up to a maximum of 130 passengers. The aircraft rapidly became a

Above: **Boeing 737-236 G-BKYK at Birmingham in 1997. This aircraft, in common with many of these early 737s, has now been retired from the British Airways fleet.** *Author*

best seller and a common sight around the world but it was not until 1978 that British Airways placed an order, initially for 19 aircraft, as part of a deal also involving the 757. Both aircraft were intended as replacements for the large fleet of Tridents inherited from BEA and which would be withdrawn from service during the 1980s.

The version chosen by British Airways was known as the 737-236 Advanced and featured several improvements as a result of in-service experience with the earlier models. These included lengthened engine nacelles incorporating thrust reversers, improved aerodynamics giving increased range, an automatic braking system, and changes to the flaps and slats to improve landing and take-off performance. In addition, the aircraft were fitted with the optional uprated JT8D-15 engines. The first 737-236 was delivered in early 1981 and a further 43 followed over the next few years, with the last being accepted in April 1985. Most were configured for scheduled services in a variable two-class layout for up to 106 passengers but several were initially allocated to British Airtours for IT work and featured a high-density 116-seat interior.

For many years these 737s formed the backbone of the short-haul fleet but as later aircraft became available they were mostly transferred to BA's Regional operations at Manchester and Birmingham, or leased to partner airlines such as GB Airways. The average age of these aircraft is now around 16 years and the old-technology JT8D engines will not meet Chapter 3 noise regulations in Europe after the year 2002 so their replacement by more modern aircraft has been inevitable. Over the past three years the fleet has been considerably reduced so that by the end of 1999 there will be only 14 in service, and the last of these will be retired by early 2001. As already related, their direct replacement is the Airbus A319 and A318. Several of the retired aircraft have found their way to other British Airways associate companies, notably Comair in South Africa, where they can be expected to give a few more years' reliable service.

When first delivered, the 737s were named after British rivers but those based at Manchester were later given titles with local connections (eg *Pride of Manchester*) while those at Birmingham carried the names of characters from Shakespearean plays.

Above: **In August 1998 British Airways announced substantial orders and options for the Airbus A320 and its derivatives, the A319 and A321. This computer-drawn image was produced by Airbus at the time and shows an A320 leading a formation with an A319 in the foreground and an A321 behind. Since that time, the Union Flag image has been adopted as the standard British Airways livery and all of the new aircraft will probably be finished in that scheme.** *Airbus Industrie*

Below: **The flightdeck of the Boeing 747-436 is typical of modern airliners with its electronic colour displays replacing conventional analogue instrumentation. This version of the 747 requires only two pilots (although relief pilots are carried on long flights) and there is no requirement for a flight engineer as carried aboard the earlier 747s. It is interesting to compare this with Concorde's flightdeck (see page 30).** *Boeing*

Above: **The Utopia livery has been widely applied to British Airways subsidiary and franchise aircraft. This Brymon Airways Dash 8 carries the Colour Down the Side image and was one of the first aircraft to be repainted in 1997.** *Bombardier Aerospace*

Below: **German subsidiary Deutsche BA has its own range of World Images drawn from various German regional inspirations. Shown here in the centre of the picture are the Bauhaus, Avignon and Calligraphy designs.** *Deutsche BA*

Boeing 737-300/400/500 (Classic)

Technical Data: Boeing 737-436
Dimensions and Weights

Length:	119ft 7in (36.45m)	Max Take-off Weight:	150,000lb (68,000kg)
Span:	94ft 10in (28.9m)	Operating Empty Weight:	73,790lb (33,470kg)
Height:	36ft 6in (11.13m)	Max Fuel:	16,137kg
Wing Area:	1,135sq ft (105.4m)		

Powerplants
Two CFM International CFM56-3C-1 turbofans; 23,500lb thrust.

Performance and Payload

Max Cruising Speed:	492kt at 26,000ft
Economic Cruising Speed:	430kt at 35,000ft
Range (Max Fuel):	2,830nm
Range (Max Payload):	1,950nm (High Gross Weight version)
Passenger Capacity:	Up to 147
Cargo Capacity:	1.74 tonnes

Left: **Although British Airways has never ordered any Boeing 737-300 series direct from Boeing, a number of this variant have found their way into the fleet at various times. This is G-OHAJ which is a leased 737-36Q based at Birmingham.** *Mike Barth*

Although superficially based on the earlier versions of the ubiquitous Boeing 737, the advanced 300/400/500 series features so many changes and improvements as to be almost a completely new aircraft. It was in 1981 that Boeing announced a new improved version of its best-selling airliner which was to be designated 737-300. The main changes were the use of new CFM56 turbofan engines together with a 7ft fuselage stretch so that up to 149 passengers could be carried in a high-density configuration. Other refinements included a strengthened undercarriage for operation at higher weights, improvements to the aerodynamics of the wing and the use of new flight management systems and electronic flight information systems derived from those developed for the larger Boeing 757. The 737-300 first flew in 1984 and airline deliveries commenced at the end of the year. In the meantime Boeing was considering a larger version which would be stretched by a further 10ft to seat up to 170 passengers and this became the 737-400 which flew in 1988. Subsequently, Boeing also introduced the 737-500 which basically retained the short fuselage of the 737-200 (then no longer in production) but incorporated all the other features of the -300 and -400. Seating up to 132 passengers, this version first flew in 1989.

British Airways placed its first order for the new Boeing 737s in October 1988 with a firm requirement for 24 aircraft and options on a further 11. This initial order was for the largest version, the 737-400, but at that stage the aircraft on option could be 300 or 500 series aircraft, as required, although neither of these variants was delivered directly from Boeing.

This original order was of great significance to Boeing as it was won against strong competition from the Airbus A320 which was already in service with British Airways and the delivery of the first aircraft, in October 1991, was of further significance as it was the 1,000th new-generation Boeing 737 to be delivered to an airline customer. Other deliveries quickly followed and 25 were in service by the spring of 1993. In British Airways service the aircraft are configured in a flexible two-class 147-seat layout and, as with the earlier 737s, are named after British rivers.

The smaller Boeing 737-300 has also been flown by British Airways on various occasions. Initially, six were leased from the Danish airline Maersk in 1988 but with the arrival of British Airways' own 737-400s, these were eventually returned. Later, when British Airways took over Dan Air in 1992 it inherited a fleet of nine 737-400s and three 737-300s which were allocated to the Gatwick-based operation. In the interests of standardisation, the 300 series aircraft were not retained although the expanding BA European operation at Gatwick continues to fly the ex-Dan Air 400 series aircraft supplemented by others from the original British Airways order. The 737-300 made a return in British Airways colours in order to plug a gap in the BA Regional fleets at Birmingham and Manchester caused by the retirement of some of the early 737-200s. A total of seven aircraft were taken on interim leases from GE Capital Aviation Services and Boullioun and these remain in service at the moment. Paradoxically, the recent large order for new Airbus aircraft has created a gap in the regional fleets as the new A318s will not be available until January 2003. In the meantime, as the last of the 737-200s are retired, their places will be temporarily taken by 100-seat 737-500s. Up to 20 of these may be acquired on five-year leases commencing from April 2000.

Boeing has now developed a new-generation 737 family comprising the 600, 700 and 800 series models. These all feature a redesigned wing, new avionics and quieter, more efficient engines as well as other detail improvements. The 737-600 equates to the previous short-fuselage 737-500; the 737-700 has the same fuselage size as the 737-300 which it replaces; while the new 737-800 is based on the 737-400 but features a longer fuselage, stretched by 2.78m to increase seating capacity to a maximum of 189 passengers. Given the recent orders placed with Airbus, it now seems unlikely that British Airways will order any of these new generation aircraft, effectively ending a long association with a very famous aircraft.

Boeing 747-200 (Classic)

Technical Data: Boeing 747-236
Dimensions and Weights

Length:	231ft 11in (70.7m)	Max Take-off Weight:	820,000lb (371,940kg)
Span:	195ft 9in (59.6m)	Operating Empty Weight:	380,800lb (172,728kg)
Height:	63ft 4in (19.3m)	Max Fuel:	164,141kg
Wing Area:	5,500sq ft (511sq m)		

Powerplants
Four Rolls-Royce RB211-524C turbofans; 51,600lb thrust.

Performance and Payload

Max Cruising Speed:	507kt at 35,000ft
Economic Cruising Speed:	490kt at 35,000ft
Range (Max Fuel):	n/a
Range (Max Payload):	6,900nm
Passenger Capacity:	373 or 425
Seating:	18 First Class, 70 Club, 285 World Traveller or 53 Club World and 372 World Traveller
Cargo Capacity:	20.3 tonnes

Above: **G-BZAW, Avro RJ100, CityFlyer Express, Union Flag.** *CityFlyer Express/John M. Dibbs*

Below: **The British Airways World Cargo Centre at Heathrow was opened in 1999. It cost £250 million to build and has the potential to handle up to 1 million tonnes of freight and cargo annually. Note the Boeing 747 freighter belonging to Japan Airlines, one of several operators flying cargo services under contract to British Airways.**
Adrian Meredith Photography via British Airways

Above: **G-BMXL, Piper PA38 Tomahawk, British Airways Flying Club, Benyhone Tartan**. *Author*

Below: **GB Airways' history of association with BEA and, more latterly with British Airways, dates back to 1947. Today it is a major franchise operator, mostly serving Spain, Gibraltar and North Africa from Gatwick, with some additional flights from Heathrow. The current fleet consists of nine Boeing 737s (G-OGBB shown here) but these will be supplemented, and eventually replaced, by Airbus A320s and A321s from 2001 onwards.** *GB Airways/John Dibbs*

The Rolls-Royce-powered Boeing 747-236 entered service with British Airways in 1977. There are now 16 of this version remaining, and it is expected that all of these will have been retired by 2002. Shown here is G-BDXO wearing the Paithani tail image. *Mike Barth*

The mighty Boeing 747 was the first of the new generation of wide-bodied airliners when it took to the air in 1969, the same year as Concorde's maiden flight. The two aircraft could hardly be more different in shape and function but, despite the technical excellence of the supersonic Concorde, it is the 747 which has changed the concept of air travel in a way which could not have been foreseen over 30 years ago. The superb seat/mile costs of the large aircraft have brought long-haul air travel within reach of virtually everybody with a consequent staggering increase in the numbers of passengers being carried. British Airways' forerunner, BOAC, was one of the first major airlines to see the potential of the new aircraft and placed orders for six aircraft as early as 1966. The first was accepted in 1970 with scheduled services commencing in April 1971 and a total of 18 747-136s had been delivered by 1976. All were powered by Pratt & Whitney JT9D-7 turbofans rated at 46,300lb thrust each. The initial configuration allowed for 358 passengers but final seating was for 18 First Class, 70 Club World and 283 World Traveller passengers, totalling 371 seats. In recent years the substantial numbers of Boeing 747-400s joining the British Airways fleet, together with the newer Boeing 777, have meant that the long-serving early 747-146 could finally be retired and the last one left the fleet in November 1999.

Following on from the early Pratt & Whitney-powered 747-136, British Airways placed orders for a Rolls-Royce-powered version of the 747-200 which, although dimensionally similar to the earlier variant, operated at much higher gross weights allowing substantial increases in range and payload. The first Rolls-Royce-powered 747-236B flew in 1976 and deliveries to British Airways commenced in the following year. Of 19 aircraft ordered, two were sold to Malaysian Airlines before delivery and an all-freighter 747-236F was sold to Cathay Pacific in 1982. The last aircraft was delivered in 1988, one of three Combi versions in the current active fleet of 16 aircraft. With a higher maximum take-off weight, British Airways configures its aircraft for 373 passengers in a three-class layout, or 425 in a two-class layout, and the maximum range is nearly 7,000 miles (11,265km), almost 2,000 miles more than could be achieved by the 747-136.

British Airways also acquired five 747-200s when it took over British Caledonian in 1987. However, these aircraft were powered by General Electric CF6 engines and consequently they were sold off at an early opportunity although, in the process, British Airways became one of the few airlines to have operated 747s powered by all three available engine marques.

Originally, many of the ex-BOAC 747-136s were named after British personalities and explorers of the Tudor and Elizabethan periods but they adopted city names after being taken over by British Airways. However, these were changed again to release the names of large cities for use on the new 747-400s and the original 100 series aircraft were then named after British lakes and inland waters, although the later 200 series are still named after major British cities (eg *City of Edinburgh*). Following the airline's recently announced intention to cut back on capacity, it would appear to be only a matter of time before the 16 747-200s are retired.

Boeing 747-400

Technical Data
Dimensions and Weights

Length:	231ft 11in (70.7m)	Max Take-off Weight:	875,000lb (396,890kg)
Span:	213ft (64.90m)	Operating Empty Weight:	390,700lb (177,218kg)
Height:	63ft 4in (19.3m)	Max Fuel:	173,520kg
Wing Area:	5,650sq ft (525sq m)		

Powerplants
Four Rolls-Royce RB211-524H turbofans; 60,300lb thrust.

Performance and Payload

Max Cruising Speed:	502kt at 35,000ft
Economic Cruising Speed:	490kt at 35,000ft
Range (Max Fuel):	8,325nm
Range (Max Payload):	6,995nm
Passenger Capacity:	386
Cargo Capacity:	20.3 tonnes

The next version of the 747 to be developed by Boeing was the 300 series which featured a distinctive extension to the upper-deck cabin to accommodate up to 44 extra passengers. This version first flew in October 1982 but was not ordered by British Airways, who preferred to wait for the technically more advanced 747-400 which first took to the air in 1988. Externally this advanced variant can be distinguished by the lengthened upper deck and winglets fitted at the wingtips. However, many major improvements are apparent only on closer inspection, the most significant being the complete redesign of the flightdeck and control systems to incorporate the latest advances in digital avionics and automated flight management systems. Much of the aircraft structure has been redesigned to incorporate new advanced alloys and composite materials and, together with more powerful engines, the maximum operating weight has

been increased to 870,800lb. British Airways aircraft are powered by Rolls-Royce RB211-524G engines which, taken with the aerodynamic and operating weight improvements, give the aircraft a maximum range of over 8,000 miles.

In 1986 British Airways signed an order for 16 747-400s (plus options on a further 12) and this order, valued at US$4.3 million, was the highest-value aircraft order ever placed up to that time. In 1990, and again in 1991, further orders and options were placed to bring the total up to 50 (88 including options) — an indication of how important the 747-400 was expected to be in the airline's fleet for the 21st century. A further 14 with upgraded RB211-524HT engines were ordered in September 1996. The first aircraft from the original order were delivered in mid-1989 and by April 1999, when the last 747 was delivered,

Left: **The Boeing 747-436 now forms the core of the British Airways long-haul fleet with no less than 57 aircraft in service. This is G-BNLA, the first of the type to be delivered, in 1989.**
Malcolm Bradbury

Above: **A British Aerospace artist's impression showing a possible 280-seater supersonic airliner which would be able to fly over much greater distances than the present Concorde, such as London to Los Angeles. However, it is becoming increasingly unlikely that such an aircraft will be built, at least not for several decades.** *British Aerospace*

Below: **All of the early Boeing 747-136s, originally ordered by BOAC, have now been retired.** *British Airways*

Right: **BAMC also carries out work for third-party airlines at Cardiff. Shown undergoing a check is an Air New Zealand Boeing 747-400 (ZK-NBT).** *Malcolm Bradbury*

a total of 57 were in service. This made British Airways the largest operator of this variant, and second only to Japan Airlines as the largest 747 operator.

A decision in 1998 to reduce capacity inevitably affected the status of the largest aircraft in the fleet and early in 1999 outstanding orders for further 747s were cancelled and replaced by additional orders for the slightly smaller and more efficient 777. It now seems unlikely that any more 747s will be delivered and indeed even some of the existing 747-400 fleet may be retired prematurely.

In British Airways service the 747-400 carries up to 409 passengers but the standard configuration is for 401 passengers in a three-class layout (14 First, 55 New Club World, 332 World Traveller). The flightdeck crew is reduced to two pilots as the digital systems do away with the need for a flight engineer although additional pilots are carried on very long sectors to allow for crew rest periods in flight. The range of the 747-400 now permits British Airways to fly nonstop to destinations such as Singapore, Hong Kong and Tokyo where flight times can be in excess of 14hr. As well as being among the most modern aircraft in the airline's fleet, the 747-400s are also the hardest working — each aircraft averaging around 4,900hr utilisation per year. Most of the 747s in the fleet are named after British cities and they are used exclusively on long air routes, mainly to North and South America, South Africa, the Far East and Australasia.

Boeing 757-236

Technical Data
Dimensions and Weights

Length:	155ft 3in (47.3m)	Max Take-off Weight:	219,801lb (99,700kg)
Span:	124ft 10in (37.90m)	Operating Empty Weight:	126,000lb (57,155kg)
Height:	45ft 6in (13.6m)	Max Fuel:	34,136kg
Wing Area:	1,994sq ft (185.25sq m)		

Powerplants
Four Rolls-Royce RB211-535C turbofans; 37,400lb thrust (or RB211-535E4; 40,100lb thrust).

Performance and Payload

Max Cruising Speed:	476kt at 37,000ft
Economic Cruising Speed:	459kt at 39,000ft
Range (Max Fuel):	4,560nm
Range (Max Payload):	3,175nm
Passenger Capacity:	180/195
Cargo Capacity:	5.8 tonnes

The Boeing 757 was developed in the 1970s in response to the massive increases in fuel costs at the beginning of the decade and was intended as a replacement for the long-serving 727 trijet. The aircraft first flew in 1982 and, powered by Rolls-Royce RB211s, it was the first time that Boeing had launched a new aircraft with non-American powerplants. The 757 was also one of the first aircraft to feature a 'glass cockpit' where the traditional rows of analogue instruments were replaced by a few electronic high-definition colour display screens and many of the routine pilot tasks were automated. British Airways was one of the launch customers (the other was Eastern Airlines) and placed firm orders for 19 with options on a further 18 in 1978. Following delivery of the first aircraft, commercial services began in 1983 and by the end of 1999 there were no less than 53 757s in the fleet. Of these, 34 are the baseline Boeing 757-236 powered by Rolls-Royce RB211-535C turbofans but from 1989 onwards the remaining aircraft were delivered with more powerful RB211-535E4 engines. This version can operate at higher gross weights and maximum range is extended by over 1,000 miles.

The arrival of the 757 in 1983 enabled British Airways to go ahead with plans to revamp and

improve its shuttle services from Glasgow, Edinburgh, Belfast and Manchester to London Heathrow in reply to competition from independent carriers such as British Midland. Replacing Trident 3B aircraft previously used, the big and quiet 757s gave a much-improved service on the now renamed 'Super Shuttle' and the aircraft dedicated to these routes have the one-class 195-seater layout. For Mainline European services, a flexible two-class layout carrying around 160 passengers is used while those aircraft employed by BA Regional on long-haul routes to the US East Coast carry 156 passengers (18 in New Club World and 138 in World Traveller). At one time the 757 was also flown by Caledonian Airways on IT charter operations carrying up to 231 passengers.

Despite the 757's long association with British Airways, it was announced in October 1999 that all of the RB211-535C-powered aircraft were to be sold back to Boeing who, in turn, would convert them to freighters for delivery to Brussels-based DHL International. In addition, a further 10 of the 535E4-powered versions would also be returned and converted. The first aircraft was flown to Boeing at the end of 1999 with the rest to follow over the next three years. They will be replaced by the recently ordered Airbus A320s (and possibly A321s), leaving only nine Boeing 757s in the British Airways fleet.

Many British Airways 757s are named after British castles, although a few operated on long-haul regional routes have names with local connotations. For example, G-BPEC flying out of Birmingham was named *Sir Simon Rattle* after the well-known conductor of the Birmingham Symphony Orchestra and G-BPEE was named *Robert Louis Stevenson* when it was first used on the Glasgow-New York route.

Boeing 767-336ER

Technical Data
Dimensions and Weights

Length:	180ft 3in (54.94m)	Max Take-off Weight:	400,000lb (181,400kg)
Span:	156ft 1in (47.57m)	Operating Empty Weight:	179,400lb (81,374kg)
Height:	52ft (15.85m)	Max Fuel:	73,078kg
Wing Area:	3,050sq ft (283.3sq m)		

Powerplants
Two Rolls-Royce RB211-524H turbofans; 60,000lb thrust.

Performance and Payload

Max Cruising Speed:	472kt at 35,000ft
Economic Cruising Speed:	460kt at 39,000ft
Range (Max Fuel):	7,180nm
Range (Max Payload):	4,900nm
Passenger Capacity:	213/252
Cargo Capacity:	Up to 12.3 tonnes

Right: **World Images: Whale Rider.** *Author*

Below: **World Images: Bauhaus.** *Author*

Bottom: **World Images: Waves and Cranes (foreground) and Koguty Lowickie.** *Author*

Left: **The Boeing 737s flown by Go have their own livery scheme with the Go logo across the tail.** *Robbie Shaw*

Below: **World Images: Colum.** *Author*

Bottom: **World Images: Waves of the City.** *Author*

The wide-bodied Boeing 767 was developed in parallel with the smaller 757 and, in fact, was the first to fly, the prototype making its maiden flight in September 1981. This initial version was the 767-200 intended for medium-range routes up to 3,000nm. It could carry a maximum of 290 passengers, although a more typical load was 216 in a two-class layout, and United Airlines was the lead customer. A 21ft 1in fuselage stretch resulted in the 767-300 version which flew in 1986 and was capable of accommodating up to 325 passengers although more realistic loads were 269 or 214 in two or three-class configuration. However, the 767 really came into its own when Extended Range versions of both the -200 and -300 were produced in 1984 and late 1986 respectively. With higher gross weights permitting the carriage of more fuel, ETOPS-approved engines and other safety-related modifications, the ER versions have proved extremely popular and account for well over half of the 967 767s ordered up to September 1999.

Despite its early commitment to the 757, British Airways was a late customer for the 767 but was the first to order a Rolls-Royce-powered version of the 767-300ER. The initial order for 11 aircraft was placed in 1987 and since then firm orders have been increased to 28 with three others on option. Deliveries began in early 1990 and all are now in service. British Airways employs the versatile 767 in two distinct roles. On high-density short-haul European routes such as London to Paris, 22 aircraft are configured in a 252-seat variable two-class layout with accommodation for up to 134 Club Europe passengers and a minimum of 95 Euro Traveller passengers. On low-density long-haul routes such as to the Gulf and the East Coast of the United States when use of larger aircraft is not warranted, the six 767s each carry a total of 213 passengers in a two-class layout with 30 New Club World and 183 World Traveller seats.

The 767 is popular with passengers, particularly in World and Euro Traveller Class where the unique 2-3-2 seating arrangement is much preferred to the more usual 3-4-3 on larger wide-bodied aircraft. Even so, they are not unaffected by plans to reduce overall capacity and at least six aircraft will be sold off, with the first (G-BNWG) being withdrawn in late 1999. Current British Airways 767s are named after European capitals and major cities.

Above: **There are currently 28 Boeing 767s in service with British Airways, but it is planned to retire at least six of these and they may possibly be leased to QANTAS. The aircraft shown is G-BNWB at Gatwick in the now standard Union Flag livery.** *Robbie Shaw*

Right: **The twinjet Boeing 777 offers significant reductions in operating costs compared to the larger 747 and is destined to play an increasingly important role in the British Airways fleet. This is G-VIIX departing from London Gatwick.** *Robbie Shaw*

Boeing 777-236

Technical Data: Boeing 777-236 (IGW)
Dimensions and Weights

Length:	209ft 1in (63.73m)	Max Take-off Weight:	590,000lb (267,600kg)
Span:	199ft 11in (60.90m)	Operating Empty Weight:	316,338lb (143,790kg)
Height:	60ft 6in (18.4m)	Max Fuel:	44,700 US gal (169,300 litres)
Wing Area:	4,605sq ft (427.8sq m)		

Powerplants
Two General Electric GE90-85B turbofans

Performance and Payload

Max Cruising Speed:	499kt at 30,000ft
Economic Cruising Speed:	484kt at 35,000ft
Range (Max Fuel):	Up to 8,000nm
Range (Max Payload):	5,500nm
Passenger Capacity:	267/380
Cargo Capacity:	39,700lb (18 tonnes)

The latest addition to the British Airways fleet is the Boeing 777, a long-range wide-bodied twinjet which first flew in June 1994. British Airways was closely involved in drawing up the specification for the 777 and placed orders for 15 aircraft (plus 15 options) in August 1990 with deliveries scheduled to begin in 1995. Surprisingly, in view of the airline's long tradition of ordering Boeing aircraft powered by Rolls-Royce, it opted for the General Electric GE90 engine although this choice was probably influenced by a simultaneous deal under which the engine manufacturer agreed to buy the British Airways engine overhaul facility in Wales for the sum of £272 million. In the event, problems with the GE90 test programme delayed delivery of the first aircraft to British Airways until 11 November 1995.

In fact, the first five aircraft, all delivered by mid-1996, were the so-called A model with a standard take-off weight of 506,000lb and optional increases up to 535,000lb giving a maximum range of 4,900nm. The remaining 10 aircraft of the original order were known as the B model which, although having the same physical dimensions, allowed take-off weights up to 590,000lb and, using higher engine-thrust ratings and carrying more fuel, enabled 325 passengers to be carried over routes up to 6,600nm. The B model subsequently became the Boeing 777-200 (IGW), the abbreviation standing for Increased Gross Weight, and these were delivered from mid-1997 onwards. When the 777 first entered service with United Airlines,

Above: **The Avro RJ100 is a derivative of the British Aerospace 146-300 from which it is externally indistinguishable. CityFlyer has 11 of this type in service or on order.** *British Aerospace*

Below: **This photo clearly shows Concorde's unique and graceful wing-form. Unlike conventional aircraft, Concorde does not have flaps and other high-lift devices, although the elevon control surfaces are drooped for landing.** *Malcolm Bradbury*

Above: **Boeing 747-436 G-BNLC taxies in the shadow of the control tower at London Gatwick. In the background is the North Terminal which opened in 1988 and is now used almost exclusively by British Airways and its associated airlines.** *Robbie Shaw*

Below: **Air Liberté also operates three DC-10-30s. To date these still retain their original livery. The example shown is F-GPVC.** *Mike Barth*

Boeing proudly claimed that it was fully certificated by the world's airworthiness authorities for ETOPS long-range flights over the oceans. In the past such status had been awarded only to airframe and engine combinations which had already shown the required level of reliability during actual airline service but in the case of the 777, Boeing and the engine manufacturers carried out an intensive test and demonstration programme in order to obtain approval for ETOPS prior to service entry. All versions of the 777 are ETOPS capable and it was intended that there would be no specific ER version although Boeing now officially designates the IGW version as the 777-200ER. A stretched version, the 737-300, first flew in October 1997 but, at the moment, British Airways has not announced any orders for this version.

Nevertheless, the 777 is destined to play an increasingly important role and by 2002 the British Airways long-haul fleet will consist of 45 B777s and 57 B747-400s, all of the 747-236s having been withdrawn by that time. Already orders and options for the 747 have been cancelled in favour of additional 777s. Currently, in addition to the original five 777-236s and 25 777-236(IGW)s, British Airways will start taking delivery of a further 15 777s powered by Rolls-Royce Trent 895 engines in January 2000. Compared to the GE-powered 777-236(IGW) which has a maximum take-off weight of 267,619kg, the Rolls-Royce version has an MTOW of 294,200kg which will substantially increase payload and range performance.

In service with British Airways, the 777 bridges the gap between the 767 and the 747-400 and has allowed the elderly DC-10s to be finally retired. The A models currently in service are configured to carry 17 passengers in First Class, 70 in New Club World and a further 148 in World Traveller making a total of 235, in addition to which up to 20 tonnes of cargo can be carried. These aircraft are used on low-volume long-haul routes to North America, the Caribbean and Gulf destinations, and are named after personalities and pioneers of aviation history such as the Wright brothers and Sir Charles Kingsford Smith. The IGW version is configured to carry 267 passengers and 18 tonnes of cargo which can be stowed in no less

than 32 standard LD3 containers. The passenger seating consists of 14 First Class in individual private cabins, 56 New Club World and 197 World Traveller. A small number of 777s are based at Gatwick where they are flown on long-haul routes to the Caribbean, Mexico and the southern United States. These aircraft are operated by Airline Management Ltd (AML) and three of the aircraft are configured in a high-density 380-seat layout aimed mainly at the IT leisure market.

Future Aircraft

Like all airlines, British Airways is constantly reviewing the size and composition of its fleet. As well as placing additional orders for existing types, it is also in a continuing dialogue with the world's major airframe and aero engine manufacturers. In this way it can ensure that its own ideas and requirements are taken into account when new aircraft are being designed and developed. In the mid-1990s the boom in air transport, particularly on long-haul routes, led to an emerging requirement for an aircraft larger than the Boeing 747-400, capable of carrying around 600 or more passengers on transoceanic and intercontinental routes. Boeing initially announced the 500X and 600X series derivatives of their very successful Boeing 747 while Airbus responded with the larger and all-new A3XX. However, Boeing appeared to have second thoughts and withdrew, leaving the field open to Airbus which is pushing ahead and intends to launch its 600-seater formally in 2000 with an in-service target date of 2005. Boeing is now looking at a more modest 747 upgrade to be known as the 747-400ER which will operate at higher gross weights and have more powerful engines. This could provide the basis for a stretched version which could carry up to 470 passengers. At one time British Airways appeared to be seriously considering the Airbus A3XX but its recent trend towards the 777 rather than the larger 747, brought about by overcapacity problems, now appears to make the possibility of an order for an ultra-large aircraft unlikely in the near future. If a large aircraft were required, the most likely candidate would appear to be the 777-300 which can carry 370/450 passengers.

For medium and short-haul routes, British Airways has gone for the Airbus A320 and its derivatives with orders and options for up to 188 aircraft to replace existing Boeing 737s and 757s. This should cover British Airways' requirements for the foreseeable future and no new type will be required in this category for some time. However, its subsidiaries Brymon Airways and CityFlyer are currently evaluating 70-110-seater jets including the Fairchild 728JET and the Airbus 318, and British Regional Airlines may also go for an aircraft of this size.

Finally, a new supersonic airliner to replace Concorde is still a possibility. Such an aircraft is under active development by a consortium of major manufacturers led by Boeing and Aérospatiale but is unlikely to be available before 2015. If and when it does fly, it will be larger than Concorde, carrying some 250 passengers in order to substantially improve seat/mile costs, and because of environmental pressures it will be much more fuel efficient and considerably less noisy. The difficulties of developing such an aircraft only serve to emphasise the technical success achieved by the British and French engineers in the 1960s when Concorde was developed and built. It is still, therefore, a matter of debate as to whether another large supersonic airliner will ever fly in British Airways colours. One practical possibility which is beginning to emerge is a small airliner version of one of the supersonic business jet projects currently under development and this would allow small groups of high-yield passengers to be flown on a variety of long-haul routes. If such an aircraft were to enter service, it would probably be affordable to most of the world's major airlines and British Airways would lose some of the prestige and glamour currently associated with its Concorde fleet.

Aircraft Operated by British Airways since 1974

Since its formation in 1974, British Airways has flown several aircraft types which are no longer represented in the current fleet. The following list gives brief details of all aircraft which have served with British Airways and its subsidiaries, British Airways Helicopters, British Airtours and Caledonian Airways, since 1974. The date of service entry and the last commercial flights are given for each type. Note that some aircraft shown as no longer in service may still be flown in British Airways colours by franchise operators. The list does not include aircraft which were operated on short-term leases from other airlines, nor those aircraft operated by BEA and BOAC but retired before the formation of British Airways. The helicopter fleet was transferred to new owners, British International Helicopters, in 1986.

Aircraft Type	In Service	Last Flown	Notes
Aérospatiale Super Puma	1983 (BAH)	1986	
Airbus A319	1999	In service	
Airbus A320	1988	In service	Ex-BCAL order
Augusta Bell Jet Ranger	1968 (BEAH)	1984	
BAC111-400/-500	1968 (BEA)	1993	
BAC/Aérospatiale Concorde	1976	In service	
BAe ATP	1989	1998	
BAe HS748	1975	1992	Highland Division
Bell 212	1978 (BAH)	1983	
Boeing 707	1960 (BOAC)	1983	
Boeing 737-200	1980	In service	
Boeing 737-300 (i)	1988	1991	Leased from Maersk
Boeing 737-300 (ii)	1992	1993	Ex-Dan Air aircraft
Boeing 737-300 (iii)	1998	In service	Leased
Boeing 737-400	1991	In service	
Boeing 747-100	1971 (BOAC)	1999	

Top: **British Regional Airlines was established in 1996, having started life as an offshoot of Manx Airlines. It is now a totally independent company with a stock exchange listing and was the first British airline to order the new generation of 50-seater regional jets, the particular example chosen being the Embraer ERJ-145.** *Embraer*

Above: **British Airways holds a 9% stake in Iberia, the Spanish flag carrier which became a member of the oneworld™ alliance in September 1999.** *Author*

Below: **Boeing 757 G-BIKW carrying the Pause to Remember logo and poppy tail image in November 1999. British Airways has now commemorated the national day of rememberence in this manner for several years.** *A. Meredith via British Airways*

Above: **A pleasing study of Boeing 767-236ER G-BZHA on approach at Heathrow. This aircraft was one of the last 767s to be delivered, in 1998, and carries the Wings image.** *Author*

Below: **G-EUPA, Airbus A319, British Airways Regional, Union Flag (wearing temporary German registration [D-AVYK] while on a test flight prior to delivery).** *Airbus Industrie*

Boeing 747-200	1977	In service	
Boeing 747-400	1989	In service	
Boeing 757-200	1983	In service	
Boeing 767-300	1990	In service	
Boeing 777-200	1995	In service	
Boeing Vertol 234 Chinook	1981	1986	
Hawker Siddeley Trident 1	1964 (BEA)	1983	
Hawker Siddeley Trident 2E	1968 (BEA)	1985	
Hawker Siddeley Trident 3B	1971 (BEA)	1985	
Lockheed L-1011 TriStar	1976	1995	
McDonnell Douglas DC-10-30	1988	1999	Ex-BCAL aircraft
Shorts SC7 Skyvan	1973 (BEA)	1977	
Sikorsky S58ET	1974	1981	
Sikorsky S61N	1964 (BEAH)	1986	
Sikorsky S76	1980	1986	
Vickers Merchantman	1969 (BEA)	1980	Cargo version of Vanguard
Vickers Vanguard	1960 (BEA)	1976	
Vickers VC10	1964 (BOAC)	1976	
Vickers Super VC10	1965 (BOAC)	1981	
Vickers Viscount	1953 (BEA)	1982	
Westland WG30	1982 (BAH)	1986	

Aircraft Flown by British Airways Subsidiary and Franchise Airlines

The advent of British Airways franchise operations in 1993 has led to a great increase in the variety of aircraft types now to be seen wearing British Airways colours and these are briefly described here.

Airbus A320
See main fleet section for details
Flown by: British Mediterranean Airlines, GB Airways (on order)

ATR42
Span: 80ft 7in (24.57m)
Length: 74ft 4in (22.67m)
Maximum Weight: 34,725lb (15,750kg)
Powerplants: Two 1,800/1,950shp Pratt & Whitney PW120/121 turboprops
Cruising Speed: 268kt (max)
Range: 1,050nm with max payload
Passenger Capacity: 48
Flown by: Air Liberté, CityFlyer Express

ATR72
Span: 88ft 9in (27.05m)
Length: 89ft 1in (27.17m)
Maximum Weight: 44,070lb (19,990kg)
Powerplants: Two 2,400shp Pratt & Whitney PW124B turboprops
Cruising Speed: 286kt (max)
Range: 645nm with max payload

Passenger Capacity: 66
Flown by: Air Liberté, CityFlyer Express, British Regional

Avro RJ100
Span: 86ft 5in (26.34m)
Length: 101ft 8in (30.99m)
Maximum Weight: 97,500lb (44,226kg)
Powerplants: Four 7,000lb thrust Allied Signal LF507-1F turbofans
Cruising Speed: 426kt
Range: 1,507nm with max payload
Passenger Capacity: 100-120
Flown by: CityFlyer Express

Boeing 727-230 Advanced
Span: 108ft (32.92m)
Length: 153ft 2in (46.69m)
Maximum Weight: 190,100lb (86,409kg)
Powerplants: Three 15,500lb thrust Pratt & Whitney JT8D-15 turbofans
Cruising Speed: 467kt
Range: 2,140nm with max payload
Passenger Capacity: 148-150
Flown by: Comair

Boeing 737-200
See main fleet section for details
Flown by: Comair

Boeing 737-300
See main fleet section for details
Flown by: Deutsche BA, GB Airways, Go Fly

Boeing 737-400
See main fleet section for details
Flown by: GB Airways

Boeing 737-500
Span: 94ft 9in (28.88m)
Length: 101ft 9in (30.01m)
Maximum Weight: 133,220lb (60,555kg)
Powerplants: Two 18,500lb thrust CFM
  International CFM56-3B1 turbofans
Cruising Speed: 492kt (max)
Range: 2,420nm (max payload)
Passenger Capacity: 114
Flown by: Maersk Air (UK)

Boeing (McDonnell Douglas) MD-83
Span: 107ft 10in (32.87m)
Length: 147ft 10in (45.06m)
Maximum Weight: 160,000lb (72,575kg)
Powerplants: Two 21,690lb thrust Pratt &
  Whitney JT8D-219 turbofans
Cruising Speed: 499kt (max)
Range: 2,500nm (max payload)
Passenger Capacity: 159
Flown by: Air Liberté

Boeing (McDonnell Douglas) DC-10-30
Span: 165ft 5in (50.40m)
Length: 182ft 1in (55.50m)
Maximum Weight: 580,000lb (263,085kg)
Powerplants: Three 52,000lb thrust General
  Electric CF6-50C2 turbofans
Cruising Speed: 490kt (max)
Range: 4,000nm (max payload)
Passenger Capacity: 329
Flown by: Air Liberté

Bombardier (Canadair) CRJ-200LR
Span: 69ft 7in (21.21m)
Length: 87ft 10in (26.77m)
Maximum Weight: 53,000lb (24,040kg)
Powerplants: Two 9,220lb thrust General
  Electric CF34-3B1 turbofans
Cruising Speed: 459kt
Range: 1,900nm with max payload
Passenger Capacity: 50
Flown by: Maersk Air UK (larger CRJ-700 also
  on order)

British Aerospace ATP
Span:100ft 6in (30.63m)
Length: 85ft 4in (26m)
Maximum Weight: 50,550lb (22,930kg)
Powerplants: Two Pratt & Whitney Canada
  PW126A turboprops; 2,388shp
Cruising Speed: 266kt (max)
Range: 575nm (with max payload)
Passenger Capacity: 64
Flown by: British Regional Airlines, Sun Air
  of Scandinavia

Above: **The turboprop ATR42, and the larger ATR72, are flown by Air Liberté and CityFlyer.** *Author*

Above: **One of the most important developments in recent years has been the formation of British Airways' own low-cost operator, Go Fly Ltd. Based at Stansted, this rapidly expanding operation is in cut-throat competition with rivals such as EasyJet and the new KLM UK subsidiary, Buzz.** *Robbie Shaw*

Below: **G-BVTK, ATR72, CityFlyer Express, Chelsea Rose.** *Robbie Shaw*

Above: **Deutsche BA is BA's German subsidiary which operates a substantial route network including many German domestic services competing directly with Lufthansa.** *Deutsche BA*

Below: **British Regional also flies the whole range of British Aerospace airliners including the BAe146, Jetstream and ATP. One of the ATPs, G-MAUD, is shown here carrying the Blue Poole tail image.** *British Aerospace*

British Aerospace BAe146 (Data for -200 series)
Span: 86ft (26.21m)
Length: 93ft 10in (28.60m)
Maximum Weight: 93,000lb (42,185kg)
Powerplants: Four 6,968lb thrust Allied Signal
  ALF502R-5 turbofans
Cruising Speed: 414kt
Range: 1,130nm with max payload
Passenger Capacity: 95
Flown by: British Regional Airlines, National
Jets Italia

British Aerospace Jetstream 31
Span: 52ft (15.85m)
Length: 47ft 2in (14.37m)
Maximum Weight: 22,377lb (10,150kg)
Powerplants: Two 940shp Allied Signal
  TPE331-10UR-513H turboprops
Cruising Speed: 260kt (max)
Range: 640nm (with max payload)
Passenger Capacity: 19
Flown by: BASE Airlines, Sun Air of
Scandinavia

British Aerospace Jetstream 41
Span: 60ft (18.29m)
Length: 63ft 2in (19.25m)
Maximum Weight: 22,377lb (10,150kg)
Powerplants: Two 1,500shp Allied Signal
  TPE331-14GR/HR turboprops
Cruising Speed: 292kt (max)
Range: 590nm (with max payload)
Passenger Capacity: 29
Flown by: British Regional Airlines, Maersk Air
UK, Sun Air of Scandinavia

De Havilland Canada DHC-6-310 Twin Otter
Span: 65ft (19.8m)
Length: 51ft 9in (15.8m)
Maximum Weight: 12,500lb (5,670kg)
Powerplants: Two 652shp Pratt & Whitney
  PT6A-27 turboprops
Cruising Speed: 182kt (max)
Range: 160nm (max payload)
Passenger Capacity: 18
Flown by: Loganair

De Havilland Canada DHC-8-300
Span: 90ft (27.43m)
Length: 84ft 3in (25.68m)

Maximum Weight: 43,000lb (19,505kg)
Powerplants: Two 2,380shp Pratt & Whitney
  PW123 turboprops
Cruising Speed: 285kt (max)
Range: 800nm (max payload)
Passenger Capacity: 48
Flown by: Brymon Airways

Embraer EMB-120ER Brasilia
Span: 64ft 11in (19.78m)
Length: 65ft 8in (20.00m)
Maximum Weight: 26,433lb (11,990kg)
Powerplants: Two 1,800shp Pratt & Whitney
  Canada PW118 turboprops
Cruising Speed: 300kt
Range: 840nm with max payload
Passenger Capacity: 28
Flown by: BASE Airlines

Embraer ERJ-145
Span: 86ft 5in (26.34m)
Length: 101ft 8in (30.99m)
Maximum Weight: 97,500lb (44,226kg)
Powerplants: Four 7,000lb thrust Allied Signal
  LF507-1F turbofans
Cruising Speed: 426kt
Range: 1,507 with max payload
Passenger Capacity: 100-120
Flown by: British Regional Airlines, Brymon
  (on order)

Fokker 100
Span: 92ft 1in (28.08m)
Length: 116ft 7in (35.53m)
Maximum Weight: 98,000lb (44,450kg)
Powerplants: Two 15,500lb thrust Rolls-Royce
  Tay 650-15 turbofans
Cruising Speed: 404kt
Range: 1,600 with max payload
Passenger Capacity: 100-120
Flown by: Air Liberté (earlier Fokker F28
  also flown)

Pilatus Britten Norman BN-2A Islander
Span: 49ft (14.94m)
Length: 35ft 8in (10.86m)
Maximum Weight: 6,600lb (2,994kg)
Powerplants: Two Lycoming O-540-E4C5
  piston engines
Cruising Speed: 140kt
Range: 250nm

Passenger Capacity: 8
Flown by: Loganair

Shorts 360
Span: 74ft 10in (22.81m)
Length: 70ft 10in (21.59m)
Maximum Weight: 27,100lb (12,292kg)
Powerplants: Two 1,424shp Pratt & Whitney
  PT6A-65AR turboprops
Cruising Speed: 210kt (max)
Range: 225nm (with max payload)
Passenger Capacity: 36
Flown by: Loganair

Notes: The De Havilland Canada DHC-7 was flown by Brymon Airways in BA Express colours but these were then replaced by the new Dash 8s. However, Brymon still retains two Dash 7s for use on oil-related contracts but these are not painted in BA colours. At one stage the CityFlyer Express fleet included a Shorts 360 in BA Express colours but this aircraft was sold. The last BAC111 in British Airways colours was operated by Maersk Air UK and was retired at the end of 1998. At the time of writing, some Air Liberté aircraft had yet to be repainted in BA colours.

Above: **The 16-seater British Aerospace Jetstream 31 has served with British Regional and Maersk UK, but the only examples now to be seen in British Airways colours are flown by the Dutch operator, BASE Airlines.** *Mike Barth*

Below: **The Shorts 360 is also flown by Loganair on inter-island services.** *Robbie Shaw*

Above: **The take-over of British Caledonian in 1988 was a significant step in the expansion of British Airways.** *Author*

Below: **Although only leased examples of the Boeing 737-300 fly with British Airways itself, this variant is also flown by Deutsche BA, GB Airways and Go. This is D-ADBQ of Deutsche BA.** *Mike Barth*

Aircraft Liveries

Airline colour schemes have come a long way since aircraft were mostly bare metal with a white cabin roof, a coloured strip down the side, and the airline name simply stated along the top of the fuselage. Today, graphic designers vie with each other in an attempt to give their clients a striking livery which will make their aircraft stand out while still giving out the required message. As Britain's flag-carrying airline, any livery which British Airways might adopt has always been cause for comment but none more so than the current 'Utopia' designs which now adorn the majority of the fleet. In creating a scheme whereby every aircraft would carry an individual design on its tail, each echoing the arts and crafts of a particular country or region, it was intended to emphasise the global nature of British Airways and to capture the imagination of its worldwide customer base.

Unfortunately, it was not seen as such by British travellers and it was famously denigrated by the former prime minister, Margaret Thatcher, at a conference only a few months after its official unveiling in the spring of 1997. In addition, it was seen as not promoting the airline's British origins and, after much pressure, it has now been decided to standardise on a single variation of the Utopia livery with a prominent Union Flag adorning the aircraft tails.

The livery worn by Britain's national airline has always been a potential cause of controversy. As far back as September 1972, when the formation of British Airways was announced, there was naturally much discussion concerning the livery which would be worn by the aircraft of the merged fleet. There was a great desire that traditional elements of the former BOAC and BEA liveries should be retained and design consultants Negus & Negus drew up a scheme which used the British national colours — red, white and blue — with a stylised and predominantly red segment of the union flag on the tail. The lower half of the fuselage was blue and the title 'British Airways' appeared on the forward cabin roof together with a modernised version of the BOAC Speedbird insignia. Wings were left natural metal although ex-BEA staff had mounted a campaign to retain the red wings which were a feature of their aircraft prior to the merger. Although one or two aircraft were painted in trial colour schemes, the first aircraft to be painted in the new official livery in 1973 was a BOAC Boeing 707 (G-AXXY) and this was followed by a BEA Trident 3 (G-AWZC) at the end of the year. Following on from this, all aircraft were gradually repainted in the new scheme although, as a temporary measure, several merely substituted the title 'British Airways' for BEA or BOAC on the cabin roof and kept their old liveries for some time.

Above: **The current British Airways livery, code-named 'Utopia', was introduced to a mixed reaction in 1997. The basic blue and white colour scheme was supplemented by individual World Images on the tail. This is Benyhone Tartan, representing Scotland, on a Boeing 757.** *Author*

The basic livery was retained for almost 10 years with no significant changes. Aircraft of the charter subsidiary adopted the same colour scheme except that they bore the title 'British Airtours' on the cabin roof. In the early 1980s there was a short-lived revision when the word 'Airways' was dropped from the titles painted on the aircraft, leaving the rather truncated 'British' in place. The rationale behind this was never fully explained or favourably received.

However, a major change of livery took place at the end of 1984 following almost two years' work by the American design consultants Landor Associates. Working in co-operation with Chester Jones, a British design bureau, they devised a new livery loosely based on the old colour scheme. This new design introduced a pearl grey tone instead of white for the upper fuselage, while the lower fuselage and engine nacelles were finished in a rich midnight blue. The stylised Union Flag on the tail was retained, although blue became the predominant colour, and the British Airways coat of arms was superimposed. The Speedbird insignia was abandoned but its shape was echoed in a diagonal slash of red forming the head of a red cheat line running down the lower fuselage.

The new livery was part of a multi-million-pound revamp of the British Airways corporate image and was extended to the fleet of vehicles and to the new uniforms and workwear for all grades of staff. The uniforms were designed by Roland Klien and the workwear, worn by engineers and ground handlers, by the House of Andre Peters. In addition, all ticketing, labelling, stationery, letterheads, logos, advertising and other details were redesigned in the new pattern which, with its combination of rich and co-ordinated colours, exuded an indefinable air of quality.

This livery stood the test of time and was admired and respected around the world. Originally, British Airtours adopted the same colours but with the take-over of British Caledonian in 1987, a new livery was adopted together with the name Caledonian. Aircraft were basically finished in the same pearl grey and midnight blue colour scheme but the fuselage cheat line was yellow and the word 'Caledonian' replaced 'British Airways' on the cabin roof, although the same Optima Bold typescript was used. The tail was all blue with the Caledonian lion rampant painted in yellow. When Caledonian was sold at the end of 1994, the new owners retained this livery which prevailed until the Caledonian name disappeared following its merger with Flying Colours at the end of 1998.

The main variation to the various British Airways liveries has been the Concorde fleet where the requirements of supersonic flight led

Above: **When first formed in 1974, British Airways adopted a red, white and blue livery with a tail pattern obviously derived from the national flag. This is illustrated on this Vickers Super VC10.** *Author's Collection*

Above: **In 1993 aircraft of the regional airlines began to adopt the standard livery with the title British Airways Express. This British Regional ATP still carried these markings as late as October 1999.** *Author*

to reduced colouring. In each case the aircraft has sported an all-white fuselage relieved originally by a thin blue cheat line and the airline title, and later by a red line and the words 'British Airways' on the forward fuselage. In both cases the standard tail markings were carried.

Other variations related to particular marketing promotions and perhaps the best known of these was 'The World's Biggest Offer' where these words, together with a representation of the Eiffel Tower and the Statue of Liberty, were painted in blue on the upper fuselage. This logo was carried by several aircraft in 1991 to publicise a marketing campaign to stimulate traffic after the downturn caused by the Gulf War. Another similar campaign was mounted in 1995 to publicise the revamp of the various brands of customer service in which the logo 'Fly New Club World' appeared on several aircraft. Other variations have included temporary markings for special flights and events including the annual 'Dreamworld' flights to Florida organised by British Airways staff for disabled children and, in 1996, a Boeing 757 had a huge poppy painted on its tail as a mark of respect for Remembrance Day on 11 November. This has subsequently been repeated in succeeding years and is now something of an annual tradition.

From 1993 a substantial number of regional aircraft began to appear in the British Airways Express livery. This was basically identical to the standard British Airways colour scheme except that the logo 'British Airways Express' was carried with the word 'Express' in normal rather than bold text. In addition, the name of the franchised airline was carried in small white letters on the nose, below the flightdeck. With the growth of the British Airways franchise scheme, the British Airways Express title was no longer applicable and has been completely dropped in the latest livery although one or two of the British Regional Airlines ATP fleet still carried these markings as late as the autumn of 1999.

By early 1997, there were strong indications that British Airways was about to introduce a new livery but the details were a closely guarded secret although by then several new aircraft had been delivered in a so-called interim livery which featured a white upper fuselage and a lighter blue on the lower fuselage and engine nacelles. The previous red 'Speedline' was omitted, the British Airways title was carried on the lower fuselage instead of the cabin roof, and a modified typescript was used. Aircraft in this interim livery carried the previous tail design in the new colour tones. It was not until June 1999 that the full colour scheme was revealed, when it caused

Each Go aircraft has a different basic colour to the standard scheme and an individual slogan on the side of the fuselage. G-IGOC has the purple variation and the words 'go today' can be seen on the forward fuselage (the other side reads 'just go'). *Terry Shone*

considerable surprise and not a little controversy. Codenamed 'Utopia', the new livery incorporated specially commissioned artworks to adorn aircraft tails while the new British Airways trademark, known as the 'Speed Marque', was applied to the upper forward fuselage. This took the form of a twisted red ribbon which vaguely echoed the shape of the original BOAC Speedbird insignia. As an aside, the word 'Speedbird' remains in everyday use today as the radio callsign prefix for all British Airways flights. As with previous livery changes, the new colour scheme was applied right across the airline's activities including ground vehicles, check-in facilities, ticketing and publicity material.

Naturally most interest centred on the tail art which was the most striking aspect of the new livery. Initially some 15 variations were announced, together with the intention to add further designs at the rate of around 12 a year until the whole fleet was repainted by the end of 2000. The cost of all this was expected to be around some £60 million and, unfortunately, the launch of the new livery coincided with a strike by some airline staff over plans to reduce expenditure in other areas by cutting jobs and other economies. Consequently, the new image got off to a bad start and the press was quick to print negative stories including one in which

it was even stated that the new colour scheme was a safety hazard because other pilots and air traffic controllers did not immediately recognise aircraft belonging to British Airways. In fact, most air traffic controllers like the new livery as it provides an easy way of identifying individual aircraft moving at busy airports such as Heathrow and Gatwick.

Utopia Liveries

The most prominent part of the Utopia livery scheme is the variety of World Image tail art designs applied to the aircraft. They are certainly colourful and interesting, if somewhat controversial, and most people seem to love them or hate them — there appears to be little room for compromise! Each image is based on traditional designs or patterns from a particular country or region, with the artist's name or signature featured in small lettering below. Subsequently, in order to make the source of inspiration more clear, the name of the country of origin was also added in more prominent lettering. Although each image has an official title, the country name is often used instead. The following list gives brief details of each of the designs used to date, arranged in order of the countries which they represent. The figure in brackets indicates the number of aircraft which carry that design (as at the end of 1999).

Water Dreaming — Australia (5)

Alternatively known as Ngapa Jukurrpa, this is the work of a major aboriginal artist called Clifford Possum Tjapaltjarri. It is centred around three grey circles representing water holes and is an interpretation of a traditional Australian Aboriginal 'Dreamtime' story.

Wunala Dreaming — Australia (2)

Another Aboriginal 'Dreamtime' interpretation which was originally applied to some QANTAS aircraft in 1994.

Nalanji Dreaming — Australia (2)

A variation of the Aboriginal 'Dreamtime' theme produced by the Balarinji Design Studio, Australia, for application to QANTAS aircraft. The mainly blue and green design is applied to two British Airways aircraft.

Animals and Trees — Botswana (Kalahari Desert) (8)

Inspired by the flora and fauna of the Kalahari Desert, artist Cg'ose Ntcox'o produced a semi-abstract design in black, red, blue and ochre depicting jackals resting under trees at an oasis.

Whale Rider — Canada (Pacific Coast) (10)

A strong design in black, red and blue, based on the painted wood carvings of the indigenous peoples of the northwest Pacific Coast. The artist, Joe David, has incorporated shapes representing a whale, serpent and a human inspired by the myths and legends of the area

Rendezvous — China (20+3)

A seemingly simple representation of traditional Chinese calligraphy which is actually an ancient poem describing the sound of water boiling in the preparation of tea. The artist was Yip Man-Yam. Although normally seen against a white background, at least three aircraft have the design on a pink background, this variation being referred to as Rendezvous Phase 2.

Wings — Denmark (13)

Artist Per Arnoldi created this image using his signature colours of red, yellow and blue, as well as white to evoke seagulls in flight over Denmark's islands. He is no stranger to the world of transport, having previously designed posters for Danish Railways.

Crossing Borders — Egypt (5)

This large image, re-creating an Egyptian scroll, combines the ancient Islamic and Pharaonic elements that are sources for the designs of the tent makers, or 'khiyamiya', of Cairo, who create multicoloured hanging panels to decorate the interiors of large tents that are erected for important events. It is the work of Cairo-based artist Chant Avedissien.

La Pyramide de Louvre — France (1)

A simple graphic depiction of the modernist pyramid structure which now forms part of the magnificent Louvre museum in Paris. It is applied to a single Air Liberté MD-83.

L'esprit Liberté — France (7)

This celebrates 50 years of the human rights movement and bears the motto, in French, which translates as 'Every Man is Born Equal and Free'. Applied only to Air Liberté aircraft.

Avignon — Germany (5)

Berlin artist Jim Avignon produced this odd painting entitled 'The men who sold the world for fun', for application to Deutsche BA aircraft.

Bauhaus (Sterntaler) — Germany (20)

A vibrant image made up of red, black and orange geometric patterns created in 1977 by Antje Bruggeman in the style of the famous Bauhaus design movement which arose in Germany after World War 1. Although applied to several of the Deutsche BA fleet, it can also be seen on the aircraft of other BA associate airlines.

Bavaria — Germany (6)

A traditional floral design, mostly in grey with red and yellow highlights, applied only to Deutsche BA aircraft. Artist Herbert Rieger drew inspiration from the art of quill embroidery in Southern Germany and Austria.

Calligraphy — Germany (4)

A Gothic-style script in grey, black and red used on some Deutsche BA aircraft. It was designed by Gottfried Pott to recall the work of the 15th-

Left: **The British Airways colour scheme is not only applied to airliners. Aircraft of the British Airways Flying Club at High Wycombe are also painted in the Utopia scheme. The photo shows Piper Warrior G-BSVG with the Colum tail image.**
Author

century German printer, Johannes Gutenberg. The name is sometimes incorrectly applied to the Chinese Rendezvous design.

Paithani — India (Maharashtra) (3)
Based on a design for a woven silk sari, this features traditional motifs including lotus flowers, swans and gold coins which in turn stem from Buddhist paintings. The artist is Meera Mehta from Bombay.

Colum (Celtic) — Ireland (22)
Based on traditional designs from the famous 9th-century *Book of Kells*, this image was created by Timothy O'Neill in memory of St Columba. *Colum* also means 'dove' in Gaelic.

Waves and Cranes — Japan (14)
A subtle blend of two repeated images by Japanese artist Matazo Kayama executed in the traditional 'Nihon-ga' style using water-based inks on hand-made paper, resulting in a complex but satisfying monochrome pattern.

Delftblue Daybreak — Netherlands (17)
Hugo Kaagman created this blue and white image which echoes the motifs still to be seen on his country's famous Delftware ceramics which have been produced since the 17th century.

Koguty Lowickie — Poland (8)
Artist Danuta Wodja created this design based on a popular Polish craft of paper cutting. The brightly coloured pattern depicts stylised cockerels, peacocks and flowers: all traditional images associated with Easter and Christmas. Some aircraft carry a variation of the basic

design which is known by the alternative name of Mazowieckie Kwiatki. These are included in the overall total.

Golden Khokhloma — Russia (3)
Khokhloma painting originated 300 years ago in the mid-Volga region of Russia, drawing on the decorative techniques of icon painters, fabric printers, jewellers, guilders, wood turners and carvers. In the unique folk art that developed, wooden utensils are covered with lavish patterns of flowers and fruit in scarlet, black and 'gold'-effect lacquer. This design is based on a set of tableware by Taisia Akimovna Belyantzev produced in 1978.

Youm-Al-Suq — Saudi Arabia (2)
Saudi Arabian female artist Shadia Alem created this stylised and vibrant abstract, with its strong colours and patterns, to conjure up an evocative picture of an Arab market.

Benyhone Tartan — Scotland (28)
Although in a traditional tartan style, this is a modern design by Peter MacDonald.

Ndebele Martha — South Africa (12)
One of a pair of complementary designs by Emmly and Martha Masanabo, two sisters from the Ndebele people of Southern Africa. The bright geometric patterns are similar to those which have been used to decorate Ndebele homes, and are based on the traditional beadwork which these people have produced for centuries, although the house painting was a 20th-century innovation. Each design bears the name of the sister who produced it, in this case Martha.

Ndebele Emmly — South Africa (3)
Emmly Masanbo's contribution to these paired designs has not been so widely adopted and is carried by only three aircraft.

Blomsterang (Flower Field) — Sweden (7)
A colourful floral design produced by Ulrica Hydman-Vallien, originally as a glass bowl. Smaland, the artist's home region, has a tradition of high-quality glassmaking going back to the 17th century.

Colour Down the Side — UK (Cornwall) (1)
This design by Cornish artist Terry Frost is seen only on a single Dash 8 flown by Brymon Airways to highlight that airline's West Country roots. Its multi-coloured streaked pattern is typical of the St Ives school.

Blue Poole — UK (8)
Poole Pottery in Dorset, England, produces distinctive ceramic ware and traces its roots back to 1861. This design by Sally Tuffin features birds and dolphins against a pale turquoise background and was originally applied to a specially commissioned vase and dish set.

British Blend — UK
In order to publicise the Utopia colour scheme, British Airways jointly sponsored a competition with the *Sunday Times* newspaper encouraging children to think of a suitable new design. The winner was 12-year-old Simon Baldwin who drew a cup of tea with English, Welsh, Scots and Irish symbols apparent in the steam rising from the traditional British 'cuppa'. It was applied only to a single Airbus A320 and that aircraft has now been repainted in the Wings scheme.

Chelsea Rose — UK (23)
Produced by Pierce Casey, this has been one of the most successful World Images and is a stylised English rose in the national colours of red, white and blue. It has been widely applied and the colour shades match well with the basic BA colour scheme.

British Olympic Association — UK (2)
The British Olympic Association 'lion' logo was designed by Mark Pickthall of Ion River Design

and rather cleverly incorporates a lion's head with a red, white and blue mane, echoing the national flag.

Grand Union — UK (5)
Another winner from a *Sunday Times* competition, artist Christine Bass drew on the traditional floral decoration applied to boats on the Grand Union Canal in the Midlands.

Pause to Remember — UK
Several aircraft have borne the red poppy motif which is used in Britain to commemorate Armistice Day in November of each year, and to remember the many millions from all nations who died in the two great wars of the 20th century. This design is usually applied on a temporary basis and is removed after a suitable period.

Union Flag — UK (74)
A bold representation of the British national flag, the Union Flag has been a national symbol for over 400 years although it first appeared in its present form in 1801 following the inclusion of the white cross of St Patrick. This design was originally known as the Chatham Flag to commemorate the flag loft at the historic Chatham dockyard which for many years was the official producer of this national symbol. Originally it was applied to only the Concorde fleet but in 1999 it was decided to adopt the design as the standard livery across the British Airways fleet and the current name was adopted.

Primavera — Romania (1)
Morag Dumitru was the winner of a competition amongst BA staff to 'design a tailfin'. Her design comes from traditionally illustrated tablecloths which the hospitable Romanians give to visitors as presents. These are typically white with red, black and blue flowers.

Waves of the City — USA (16)
A 1994 wave-like abstract design by American artist Jennifer Kobylarz. Mostly in white and two shades of blue, with red and green highlights.

4. British Airways Combined Fleet List

The following is a list of all aircraft operated by British Airways, its subsidiaries and franchise operators. This list is in order of aircraft registration and indicates the type of aircraft, World Image colour scheme (if appropriate), aircraft name, operator and any relevant notes. In the column labelled 'Fleet', these abbreviations apply:

BA — British Airways Mainline fleet
BA Regional (MAN) — British Airways Regional (Manchester)
BA Regional (BHX) — British Airways Regional (Birmingham)
BA (Euro LGW) — British Airways European Operations at Gatwick

Absence of an entry under 'Colours' normally indicates that the aircraft concerned has yet to be painted in the Utopia livery.
Details given are believed correct as at 1 April 2000.

Reg	Type	Colours	Name	Fleet	Notes
D-ADBA	Boeing 737-3L9	Avignon	Metropolis	Deutsche BA	
D-ADBB	Boeing 737-3L9			Deutsche BA	
D-ADBC	Boeing 737-3L9	Bavaria	Enzian	Deutsche BA	
D-ADBD	Boeing 737-3L9			Deutsche BA	
D-ADBE	Boeing 737-3L9	Bauhaus	Sterntaler	Deutsche BA	
D-ADBF	Boeing 737-3L9	Bavaria	Windrose	Deutsche BA	
D-ADBG	Boeing 737-3L9	Bavaria	Edelweiss	Deutsche BA	
D-ADBH	Boeing 737-3L9	Bavaria	Bavaria	Deutsche BA	
D-ADBI	Boeing 737-3L9	Avignon	Phantasia	Deutsche BA	
D-ADBK	Boeing 737-300	Bauhaus	Aurora	Deutsche BA	
D-ADBL	Boeing 737-300	Bauhaus	Himmelstürmer	Deutsche BA	
D-ADBM	Boeing 737-300	Calligraphy	Schrifttanz	Deutsche BA	
D-ADBN	Boeing 737-300	Calligraphy	Wolkenschreiber	Deutsche BA	
D-ADBO	Boeing 737-300	Calligraphy	Himmelsbrief	Deutsche BA	
D-ADBP	Boeing 737-300	Calligraphy	Federtraum	Deutsche BA	
D-ADBQ	Boeing 737-300	Avignon	Paradiesvogel	Deutsche BA	
D-ADBR	Boeing 737-300	Bauhaus	Sternschnuppe	Deutsche BA	
D-ADBS	Boeing 737-300	Bauhaus	Rheingold	Deutsche BA	
D-ADBT	Boeing 737-300	Avignon	Phantasia	Deutsche BA	
D-ADBU	Boeing 737-300	Avignon	Metropolis	Deutsche BA	
D-ADBV	Boeing 737-31S	Bauhaus	Sterntaler	Deutsche BA	
D-ADBW	Boeing 737-31S	Bauhaus	Wolkenreiter	Deutsche BA	
D-ADIA	Boeing 737-300	Bavaria		Deutsche BA	
D-ADIB	Boeing 737-300	Bavaria		Deutsche BA	
D-ADIC	Boeing 737-300	Bavaria		Deutsche BA	
F-GDUS	Fokker F28-2000			Air Liberté	
F-GDUT	Fokker F28-2000			Air Liberté	
F-GDUU	Fokker F28-2000			Air Liberté	
F-GDUV	Fokker F28-2000			Air Liberté	
F-GFZB	MD-83			Air Liberté	
F-GGLK	ATR42-300			Air Liberté	
F-GHEB	MD-83	L'esprit Liberté		Air Liberté	
F-GHED	MD-83			Air Liberté	
F-GHEI	MD-83			Air Liberté	
F-GHEK	MD-83			Air Liberté	
F-GHHO	MD-83			Air Liberté	
F-GHHP	MD-83			Air Liberté	
F-GIOA	Fokker 100			Air Liberté	
F-GIOG	Fokker 100	L'esprit Liberté		Air Liberté	
F-GIOH	Fokker 100			Air Liberté	
F-GIOI	Fokker 100	L'esprit Liberté		Air Liberté	
F-GIOJ	Fokker 100			Air Liberté	

Reg	Type	Colours	Name	Fleet	Notes
F-GIOK	Fokker 100			Air Liberté	
F-GIRC	ATR42-300			Air Liberté	
F-GJHQ	MD-83			Air Liberté	
F-GKNB	ATR42-300			Air Liberté	
F-GKNC	ATR42-300			Air Liberté	
F-GKND	ATR42-300			Air Liberté	
F-GKOA	ATR72-202			Air Liberté	
F-GKOB	ATR72-202	L'esprit Liberté		Air Liberté	
F-GNLG	Fokker 100			Air Liberté	
F-GNLH	Fokker 100			Air Liberté	
F-GNLI	Fokker 100			Air Liberté	
F-GNLJ	Fokker 100			Air Liberté	
F-GNLK	Fokker 100			Air Liberté	
F-GPVA	DC-10-30	L'esprit Liberté		Air Liberté	
F-GPVC	DC-10-30(ER)			Air Liberté	
F-GPVD	DC-10-30			Air Liberté	
F-GPZA	MD-83	Pyramide		Air Liberté	
F-GRML	MD-83	L'esprit Liberté		Air Liberté	
G-BDXA	Boeing 747-236B		City of Peterborough	BA	
G-BDXB	Boeing 747-236B	Nigeria Airways	City of Liverpool	BA	Leased to Nigeria Airways
G-BDXC	Boeing 747-236B		City of Manchester	BA	
G-BDXE	Boeing 747-236B		City of Glasgow	BA	
G-BDXF	Boeing 747-236B		City of York	BA	
G-BDXG	Boeing 747-236B	Blomsterang	City of Oxford	BA	
G-BDXH	Boeing 747-236B		City of Elgin	BA	
G-BDXI	Boeing 747-236B		City of Cambridge	BA	
G-BDXJ	Boeing 747-236B		City of Birmingham	BA	
G-BDXK	Boeing 747-236B	Chelsea Rose	City of Canterbury	BA	
G-BDXL	Boeing 747-236B		City of Winchester	BA	
G-BDXM	Boeing 747-236B (SCD)		City of Derby	BA	
G-BDXN	Boeing 747-236B (SCD)		City of Stoke on Trent	BA	
G-BDXO	Boeing 747-236B	Paithani	City of Bath	BA	
G-BDXP	Boeing 747-236B (SCD)		City of Salisbury	BA	
G-BGDA	Boeing 737-236	Ndebele Martha	Bridgewater	BA (Euro LGW)	Disposal 21/02/2001
G-BGDE	Boeing 737-236	Bauhaus	River Avon	BA (Euro LGW)	Disposal 07/02/2001
G-BGDF	Boeing 737-236	Delftblue Daybreak	River Thames	BA (Euro LGW)	Disposal 17/01/2001
G-BGDJ	Boeing 737-236	Waves & Cranes	Delamare Forest	BA Regional BHX	Disposal 26/03/01
G-BGDL	Boeing 737-236	Benyhone Tartan	River Don	BA (Euro LGW)	Disposal 07/03/2001
G-BGDO	Boeing 737-236	Whale Rider	River Usk	BA Regional BHX	Disposal 30/09/00
G-BGDR	Boeing 737-236	Colum (Celtic)	River Bann	BA (Euro LGW)	Disposal 11/04/2001
G-BGDT	Boeing 737-236	Animals & Trees	Wirral Peninsula	BA Regional BHX	Disposal 16/05/01
G-BGJE	Boeing 737-236	Rendezvous	River Wear	BA (Euro LGW)	Disposal 31/10/2000
G-BIKA	Boeing 757-236	Blue Poole	Dover Castle	BA	Disposal 06/00
G-BIKB	Boeing 757-236	Chelsea Rose	Windsor Castle	BA	
G-BIKC	Boeing 757-236	Ndebele Emmly	Edinburgh Castle	BA	
G-BIKD	Boeing 757-236		Caernafon Castle	BA	
G-BIKF	Boeing 757-236	Wunala Dreaming	Carrickfergus Castle	BA	
G-BIKH	Boeing 757-236	Golden Khokhloma	Richmond Castle	BA	
G-BIKI	Boeing 757-236	Rendezvous	Tintagel Castle	BA	
G-BIKJ	Boeing 757-236	Waves of the City	Conwy Castle	BA	
G-BIKK	Boeing 757-236		Eilean Donan Castle	BA	
G-BIKL	Boeing 757-236	Benyhone Tartan	Nottingham Castle	BA	
G-BIKM	Boeing 757-236		Glamis Castle	BA	
G-BIKN	Boeing 757-236	Rendezvous	Bodiam Castle	BA	
G-BIKO	Boeing 757-236	Benyhone Tartan	Harlech Castle	BA	
G-BIKP	Boeing 757-236		Enniskillen Castle	BA	
G-BIKR	Boeing 757-236	Union Flag	Bamburgh Castle	BA	
G-BIKS	Boeing 757-236		Corfe Castle	BA	
G-BIKT	Boeing 757-236	Crossing Borders	Carisbrooke Castle	BA	
G-BIKU	Boeing 757-236		Inveraray Castle	BA	
G-BIKV	Boeing 757-236	Union Flag	Raglan Castle	BA	
G-BIKW	Boeing 757-236	Union Flag	Belvoir Castle	BA	

Reg	Type	Colours	Name	Fleet	Notes
G-BIKX	Boeing 757-236	Delftblue Daybreak	*Warwick Castle*	BA	
G-BIKY	Boeing 757-236	Primavera	*Leeds Castle*	BA	
G-BIKZ	Boeing 757-236	Union Flag	*Kenilworth Castle*	BA	
G-BJOP	BN-2B-26 Islander	Colum (Celtic)	*Capt E. E. Fresson OBE*	Loganair	
G-BKMX	Shorts 360-100			Loganair	
G-BKYH	Boeing 737-236		*Hotspur*	BA Regional BHX	
G-BKYP	Boeing 737-236	Waves & Cranes	*River Ystwyth*	BA Regional MAN	
G-BLDV	BN-2B-26 Islander	Benyhone Tartan	*Sir James Young Simpson*	Loganair	
G-BLGB	Shorts 360-100			Loganair	
G-BLNJ	BN-2B-26 Islander	Ndebele Martha	*E. L. Gander Dower Esq*	Loganair	
G-BLNW	BN-2B-26 Islander		*Sister Jean Kennedy*	Loganair (Scottish Air Ambulance)	
G-BMAR	Shorts 360-100			Loganair	
G-BMRA	Boeing 757-236	Paithani	*Beaumaris Castle*	BA	
G-BMRB	Boeing 757-236	Union Flag	*Colchester Castle*	BA	
G-BMRC	Boeing 757-236	British Olympic Ass'n	*Rochester Castle*	BA	
G-BMRD	Boeing 757-236	Chelsea Rose	*Bothwell Castle*	BA	
G-BMRE	Boeing 757-236	Rendezvous	*Killyleagh Castle*	BA	
G-BMRF	Boeing 757-236	Water Dreaming	*Hever Castle*	BA	
G-BMRG	Boeing 757-236	Rendezvous	*Caerphilly Castle*	BA	
G-BMRH	Boeing 757-236	Nalanji Dreaming	*Norwich Castle*	BA	
G-BMRI	Boeing 757-236	Blomsterang	*Tonbridge Castle*	BA	
G-BMRJ	Boeing 757-236	Grand Union	*Loch Tummel*	BA	
G-BMVL	Piper PA38	Blue Poole		BA Flying Club	
G-BMVM	Piper PA38	Waves of the City		BA Flying Club	
G-BMXL	Piper PA38	Benyhone Tartan		BA Flying Club	
G-BNCR	Piper PA28	Chelsea Rose		BA Flying Club	
G-BNLA	Boeing 747-436	Chelsea Rose	*City of London*	BA	
G-BNLB	Boeing 747-436	Union Flag	*City of Edinburgh*	BA	
G-BNLC	Boeing 747-436	Colum (Celtic)	*City of Cardiff/Dinas Caerdydd*	BA	
G-BNLD	Boeing 747-436	Delftblue Daybreak	*City of Belfast*	BA	
G-BNLE	Boeing 747-436	Union Flag	*City of Newcastle*	BA	
G-BNLF	Boeing 747-436	Union Flag	*City of Leeds*	BA	
G-BNLG	Boeing 747-436	Whale Rider	*City of Southampton*	BA	
G-BNLH	Boeing 747-436	Wings	*City of Westminster*	BA	
G-BNLI	Boeing 747-436	Benyhone Tartan	*City of Sheffield*	BA	
G-BNLJ	Boeing 747-436	Ndebele Martha	*City of Nottingham*	BA	
G-BNLK	Boeing 747-436	Water Dreaming	*City of Bristol*	BA	
G-BNLL	Boeing 747-436	Chelsea Rose	*City of Leicester*	BA	
G-BNLM	Boeing 747-436	Ndebele Martha	*City of Durham*	BA	
G-BNLN	Boeing 747-436	Nalanji Dreaming	*City of Portsmouth*	BA	
G-BNLO	Boeing 747-436	Ndebele Emmly	*City of Dundee*	BA	
G-BNLP	Boeing 747-436	Union Flag	*City of Aberdeen*	BA	
G-BNLR	Boeing 747-436	Rendezvous	*City of Hull*	BA	
G-BNLS	Boeing 747-436	Wunala Dreaming	*City of Chester*	BA	
G-BNLT	Boeing 747-436	Koguty Lowickie	*City of Lincoln*	BA	
G-BNLU	Boeing 747-436		*City of Bangor*	BA	
G-BNLV	Boeing 747-436	Waves of the City	*City of Exeter*	BA	
G-BNLW	Boeing 747-436		*City of Norwich*	BA	
G-BNLX	Boeing 747-436	Waves of the City	*City of Worcester*	BA	
G-BNLY	Boeing 747-436	Union Flag	*City of Swansea*	BA	
G-BNLZ	Boeing 747-436	Animals & Trees	*City of Perth*	BA	
G-BNMT	Shorts 360	Koguty Lowickie	*Cockerel of Lowicz*	Loganair	
G-BNMU	Shorts 360	Colum (Celtic)		Loganair	
G-BNMW	Shorts 360	Delftblue Daybreak		Loganair	
G-BNNK	Boeing 737-4Q8	Waves of the City	*Mons Chambi (Tunisia)*	GB Airways	
G-BNNL	Boeing 737-4Q8	Chelsea Rose	*Mons Ben Nevis (UK)*	GB Airways	
G-BNWA	Boeing 767-336ER	Delftblue Daybreak	*City of Brussels*	BA	
G-BNWB	Boeing 767-336	Chelsea Rose	*City of Paris*	BA	
G-BNWC	Boeing 767-336	Rendezvous	*City of Frankfurt*	BA	
G-BNWD	Boeing 767-336	Ndebele Martha	*City of Copenhagen*	BA	
G-BNWE	Boeing 767-336	Chelsea Rose	*City of Lisbon*	BA	To QANTAS 06/00
G-BNWF	Boeing 767-336	Benyhone Tartan	*City of Milan*	BA	To QANTAS 06/00

Reg	Type	Colours	Name	Fleet	Notes
G-BNWH	Boeing 767-336ER	Union Flag	*City of Rome*	BA	
G-BNWI	Boeing 767-336ER		*City of Madrid*	BA	
G-BNWJ	Boeing 767-336	Golden Khokhloma	*City of Athens*	BA	To QANTAS 06/00
G-BNWK	Boeing 767-336	Colum (Celtic)	*City of Amsterdam*	BA	To QANTAS 06/00
G-BNWL	Boeing 767-336	Union Flag	*City of Luxembourg*	BA	To QANTAS 06/00
G-BNWM	Boeing 767-336ER		*City of Toulouse*	BA	
G-BNWN	Boeing 767-336ER		*City of Berlin*	BA	
G-BNWO	Boeing 767-336ER		*City of Barcelona*	BA	
G-BNWP	Boeing 767-336	Rendezvous	*City of Dublin*	BA	To QANTAS 06/00
G-BNWR	Boeing 767-336ER	Union Flag	*City of Hamburg*	BA	
G-BNWS	Boeing 767-336		*City of Oporto*	BA	
G-BNWT	Boeing 767-336	Benyhone Tartan	*City of Cork*	BA	
G-BNWU	Boeing 767-336ER	Blomsterang	*Robert Burns*	BA	
G-BNWV	Boeing 767-336	Colum (Celtic)	*City of Bonn*	BA	
G-BNWW	Boeing 767-336	Union Flag	*City of Marseille*	BA	
G-BNWX	Boeing 767-336	Union Flag	*City of Bilbao*	BA	
G-BNWY	Boeing 767-336	Union Flag	*City of Helsinki*	BA	
G-BNWZ	Boeing 767-336	Union Flag		BA	
G-BOAA	BAe/Aérospatiale Concorde 102	Union Flag		BA	
G-BOAB	BAe/Aérospatiale Concorde 102	Union Flag		BA	
G-BOAC	BAe/Aérospatiale Concorde 102	Union Flag		BA	
G-BOAD	BAe/Aérospatiale Concorde 102	Union Flag		BA	
G-BOAE	BAe/Aérospatiale Concorde 102	Union Flag		BA	
G-BOAF	BAe/Aérospatiale Concorde 102	Union Flag		BA	
G-BOAG	BAe/Aérospatiale Concorde 102	Union Flag		BA	
G-BODR	Piper PA28	Waves & Cranes		BA Flying Club	
G-BPCA	BN-2B-26 Islander		*Capt David Barclay MBE*	Loganair (Scottish Air Ambulance)	
G-BPEA	Boeing 757-236	Union Flag	*Kidwelly Castle*	BA	
G-BPEB	Boeing 757-236	Union Flag		BA	
G-BPEC	Boeing 757-236	Waves & Cranes	*Sir Simon Rattle*	BA	
G-BPED	Boeing 757-236	Koguty Lowickie	*Blair Castle*	BA	
G-BPEE	Boeing 757-236	Union Flag	*Robert Louis Stevenson*	BA	
G-BPEF	Boeing 757-236			BA	
G-BPEI	Boeing 757-236	Union Flag	*Winchester Castle*	BA	
G-BPEJ	Boeing 757-236	Union Flag	*Castell Dinas Bran*	BA	
G-BPEK	Boeing 757-236	Union Flag	*Carew Castle*	BA	
G-BPFN	Shorts 360	Benyhone Tartan		Loganair	
G-BRJA	Embraer ERJ-145			Brymon	Del 02/2000
G-BRJB	Embraer ERJ-145			Brymon	Del 03/2000
G-BRJC	Embraer ERJ-145			Brymon	Del 2000
G-BRJD	Embraer ERJ-145			Brymon	Del 2000
G-BRJE	Embraer ERJ-145			Brymon	Del 2000
G-BRJF	Embraer ERJ-145			Brymon	Del 2000
G-BRJG	Embraer ERJ-145			Brymon	Del 2001
G-BRYA	DHC Dash 7-100	Not BA colours	*Aberdeen/Obar Dhethian*	Brymon Offshore	
G-BRYD	DHC Dash 7-100	Not BA colours	*Cornwall/Kernow*	Brymon Offshore	
G-BRYJ	DHC Dash 8-311	Grand Union	*Somerset/Gwiad Yr Haf*	Brymon Offshore	
G-BRYM	DHC Dash 8-311			Brymon	For disposal 1999
G-BRYO	DHC Dash 8-311		*Harveys*	Brymon	
G-BRYP	DHC Dash 8-311	Grand Union		Brymon	
G-BRYR	DHC Dash 8-311		*English China Clay*	Brymon	
G-BRYS	DHC Dash 8-311	Waves of the City		Brymon	
G-BRYT	DHC Dash 8-311	Colour Down the Side		Brymon	
G-BRYU	DHC Dash 8-311	Benyhone Tartan		Brymon	
G-BRYV	DHC Dash 8-311	Colum (Celtic)		Brymon	

Reg	Type	Colours	Name	Fleet	Notes
G-BRYW	DHC Dash 8-311	Koguty Lowickie		Brymon	
G-BRYX	DHC Dash 8-311	All White		Brymon	
G-BRYY	DHC Dash 8-311	Rendezvous		Brymon	
G-BRYZ	DHC Dash 8-311	All White		Brymon	
G-BSNV	Boeing 737-4Q8			BA (Euro LGW)	Leased from IFLC
G-BSNW	Boeing 737-4Q8	Union Flag		BA (Euro LGW)	Leased from IFLC
G-BSSX	Piper PA28	Union Flag		BA Flying Club	
G-BSVG	Piper PA28	Colum (Celtic)		BA Flying Club	
G-BUEA	ATR42-310	Union Flag		CityFlyer Express	For Disposal
G-BUHJ	Boeing 737-4Q8			BA (Euro LGW)	Leased from IFLC
G-BUHK	Boeing 737-4Q8	Union Flag		BA (Regional Man)	Leased from IFLC
G-BUHL	Boeing 737-4Q8	Wings	Mons Veleta (Spain)	GB Airways	
G-BUSB	Airbus A320-111	Koguty Lowickie	Isle of Jersey	BA	
G-BUSC	Airbus A320-111	British Olympic Ass'n	Isle of Skye	BA	
G-BUSD	Airbus A320-111		Isle of Mull	BA	
G-BUSE	Airbus A320-111	Benyhone Tartan	Isles of Scilly	BA	
G-BUSF	Airbus A320-111		Isle of Man	BA	
G-BUSG	Airbus A320-211	Bauhaus	Isle of Wight	BA	
G-BUSH	Airbus A320-211		Isle of Jura	BA	
G-BUSI	Airbus A320-211	Union Flag	Isle of Anglesey	BA	
G-BUSJ	Airbus A320-211	Water Dreaming	Isle of Sark	BA	
G-BUSK	Airbus A320-211	Waves & Cranes	Isle of Guernsey	BA	
G-BVEC	ATR42-310			CityFlyer Express	
G-BVED	ATR42-310			CityFlyer Express	
G-BVEF	ATR42-310	Union Flag		CityFlyer Express	
G-BVMY	Shorts 360	Delftblue Daybreak		Loganair	
G-BVNM	Boeing 737-4S3	Union Flag		BA (Euro LGW)	
G-BVNN	Boeing 737-4S3	Union Flag		BA (Euro LGW)	
G-BVNO	Boeing 737-4S3	Benyhone Tartan		BA (Euro LGW)	
G-BVTJ	ATR72-202	Waves & Cranes		CityFlyer Express	
G-BVTK	ATR72-202	Chelsea Rose		CityFlyer Express	
G-BVVK	DHC-6 Twin Otter 310			Loganair	
G-BWTL	ATR72-202	Union Flag		CityFlyer Express	
G-BWTM	ATR72-202	Benyhone Tartan		CityFlyer Express	
G-BXAR	Avro RJ100	Delftblue Daybreak		CityFlyer Express	
G-BXAS	Avro RJ100	Animals & Trees		CityFlyer Express	
G-BXEG	ATR42-310	Union Flag		CityFlyer Express	
G-BXGL	DHC-1 Chipmunk	(BOAC Colours)		BA Flying Club	
G-BXTN	ATR72-202	Whale Rider		CityFlyer Express	
G-BXPZ	DHC Dash 8-311	All white		Brymon	
G-BYGA	Boeing 747-436	Chelsea Rose		BA	
G-BYGB	Boeing 747-436	Colum (Celtic)		BA	
G-BYGC	Boeing 747-436	Chelsea Rose		BA	
G-BYGD	Boeing 747-436	Rendezvous		BA	
G-BYGE	Boeing 747-436	Rendezvous		BA	
G-BYGF	Boeing 747-436	Chelsea Rose		BA	
G-BYGG	Boeing 747-436	Rendezvous		BA	
G-BYTO	ATR72-210	Union Flag		CityFlyer Express	Leased
G-BYTP	ATR72-210	Colum (Celtic)		CityFlyer Express	Leased
G-BZAT	Avro RJ100	Waves of the City		CityFlyer Express	
G-BZAU	Avro RJ100	Colum (Celtic)		CityFlyer Express	
G-BZAV	Avro RJ100	Chelsea Rose		CityFlyer Express	
G-BZAW	Avro RJ100	Union Flag		CityFlyer Express	
G-BZAX	Avro RJ100	Union Flag		CityFlyer Express	
G-BZAY	Avro RJ100	Union Flag		CityFlyer Express	Due 03/2000
G-BZAZ	Avro RJ100	Union Flag		CityFlyer Express	Due 04/2000
G-BZHA	Boeing 767-336	Wings		BA	
G-BZHB	Boeing 767-336	Delftblue Daybreak		BA	
G-BZHC	Boeing 767-336	Waves & Cranes		BA	
G-CFAA	Avro RJ100	Union Flag		CityFlyer Express	Del 06/00
G-CIVA	Boeing 747-436	Chelsea Rose	City of St Davids/Dinas Tyddewi	British Asia	
G-CIVB	Boeing 747-436	Chelsea Rose	City of Lichfield	British Asia	

Reg	Type	Colours	Name	Fleet	Notes
G-CIVC	Boeing 747-436	Delftblue Daybreak	*City of St Andrews*	BA	
G-CIVD	Boeing 747-436	Waves of the City	*City of Coventry*	BA	
G-CIVE	Boeing 747-436	Union Flag	*City of Sunderland*	BA	
G-CIVF	Boeing 747-436		*City of St Albans*	BA	
G-CIVG	Boeing 747-436		*City of Wells*	BA	
G-CIVH	Boeing 747-436		*City of Hereford*	BA	
G-CIVI	Boeing 747-436		*City of Gloucester*	BA	
G-CIVJ	Boeing 747-436			BA	
G-CIVK	Boeing 747-436			BA	
G-CIVL	Boeing 747-436			BA	
G-CIVM	Boeing 747-436	Waves & Cranes		BA	
G-CIVN	Boeing 747-436	Delftblue Daybreak		BA	
G-CIVO	Boeing 747-436	Benyhone Tartan		BA	
G-CIVP	Boeing 747-436	Colum (Celtic)		BA	
G-CIVR	Boeing 747-436	Waves & Cranes		BA	
G-CIVS	Boeing 747-436	Whale Rider		BA	
G-CIVT	Boeing 747-436	Delftblue Daybreak		BA	
G-CIVU	Boeing 747-436	Wings		BA	
G-CIVV	Boeing 747-436	Rendezvous		BA	
G-CIVW	Boeing 747-436	Benyhone Tartan		BA	
G-CIVX	Boeing 747-436	Union Flag		BA	
G-CIVY	Boeing 747-436	Whale Rider		BA	
G-CIVZ	Boeing 747-436	Benyhone Tartan		BA	
G-CPEL	Boeing 757-236	Animals & Trees	*Walmer Castle*	BA	
G-CPEM	Boeing 757-236	Blue Poole		BA	
G-CPEN	Boeing 757-236	Union Flag		BA	
G-CPEO	Boeing 757-236	Whale Rider		BA	
G-CPEP	Boeing 757-236	Colum (Celtic)		BA	
G-CPER	Boeing 757-236	Wings		BA	
G-CPES	Boeing 757-236	Wings		BA	
G-CPET	Boeing 757-236	Bauhaus (Sterntaler)		BA	
G-CPEU	Boeing 757-236	Rendezvous		BA	
G-CPEV	Boeing 757-236	Rendezvous		BA	
G-DOCA	Boeing 737-436	Benyhone Tartan	*River Ballinderry*	BA (Euro LGW)	
G-DOCB	Boeing 737-436	Wings	*River Bush*	BA	
G-DOCC	Boeing 737-436	Blue Poole	*River Afric*	BA	
G-DOCD	Boeing 737-436	Animals & Trees	*River Aire*	BA	
G-DOCF	Boeing 737-436	Blomsterang	*River Alness*	BA	
G-DOCF	Boeing 737-436	Koguty Lowickie	*River Beaully*	BA (Euro LGW)	
G-DOCG	Boeing 737-436	Chelsea Rose	*River Blackwater*	BA (Euro LGW)	
G-DOCH	Boeing 737-436	Grand Union	*River Brue*	BA (Euro LGW)	
G-DOCI	Boeing 737-436	Union Flag	*River Carron*	BA (Euro LGW)	
G-DOCJ	Boeing 737-436	Benyhone Tartan	*River Glass*	BA (Euro LGW)	
G-DOCK	Boeing 737-436	Union Flag	*River Lochay*	BA (Euro LGW)	
G-DOCL	Boeing 737-436	Ndebele Martha	*River Lune*	BA (Euro LGW)	
G-DOCM	Boeing 737-436	Rendezvous	*River Meon*	BA (Euro LGW)	
G-DOCN	Boeing 737-436	Union Flag	*River Ottery*	BA (Euro LGW)	
G-DOCO	Boeing 737-436		*River Parrett*	BA (Euro LGW)	
G-DOCP	Boeing 737-436	Union Flag	*River Swift*	BA (Euro LGW)	
G-DOCR	Boeing 737-436	Waves of the City	*River Tavy*	BA (Euro LGW)	
G-DOCS	Boeing 737-436		*River Teifi*	BA (Euro LGW)	
G-DOCT	Boeing 737-436	Crossing Borders	*River Tene*	BA (Euro LGW)	
G-DOCU	Boeing 737-436	Ndebele Martha	*River Teviot*	BA	
G-DOCV	Boeing 737-436	Benyhone Tartan	*River Thurso*	BA	
G-DOCW	Boeing 737-436	Rendezvous	*Co of Bedfordshire*	BA (Euro LGW)	
			-Cranfield University	BA (Euro LGW)	
G-DOCX	Boeing 737-436	Colum (Celtic)	*River Tirry*	BA (Euro LGW)	
G-DOCY	Boeing 737-436		*River Weaver*	BA (Euro LGW)	
G-DOCZ	Boeing 737-436			BA (Euro LGW)	
G-EMBA	ERJ-145	Colum (Celtic)		Br Regional Airlines	
G-EMBB	ERJ-145	Bauhaus		Br Regional Airlines	
G-EMBC	ERJ-145	Koguty Lowickie		Br Regional Airlines	

Reg	Type	Colours	Name	Fleet	Notes
G-EMBD	ERJ-145	Animals & Trees		Br Regional Airlines	
G-EMBE	ERJ-145	Waves of the City		Br Regional Airlines	
G-EMBF	ERJ-145	Grand Union		Br Regional Airlines	
G-EMBG	ERJ-145	Water Dreaming		Br Regional Airlines	
G-EMBH	ERJ-145	Blomsterang		Br Regional Airlines	
G-EMBI	ERJ-145	Paithani		Br Regional Airlines	
G-EMBJ	ERJ-145	Youm-Al-Suq		Br Regional Airlines	
G-EMBK	ERJ-145	Benyhone Tartan		Br Regional Airlines	
G-EMBL	ERJ-145	Union Flag		Br Regional Airlines	
G-EMBM	ERJ-145	Union Flag		Br Regional Airlines	
G-EMBN	ERJ-145			Br Regional Airlines	Del 01/00
G-EMBO	ERJ-145			Br Regional Airlines	Del 03/00
G-EORG	Piper PA38	Whale Rider		BA Flying Club	
G-ERJA	ERJ-145	Union Flag		Brymon	
G-ERJB	ERJ-145	Union Flag		Brymon	
G-ERJC	ERJ-145	-		Brymon	Del 2000
G-ERJD	ERJ-145	-		Brymon	Del 2000
G-ERJE	ERJ-145	-		Brymon	Del 2000
G-ERJF	ERJ-145	-		Brymon	Del 2001
G-ERJG	ERJ-145	-		Brymon	Del 2001
G-EUOA	Airbus A320			BA Regional	Del 2001
G-EUOB	Airbus A320			BA Regional	On Order
G-EUOC	Airbus A320			BA Regional	On Order
G-EUOD	Airbus A320			BA Regional	On Order
G-EUOE	Airbus A320			BA Regional	On Order
G-EUOF	Airbus A320			BA Regional	On Order
G-EUOG	Airbus A320			BA Regional	On Order
G-EUOH	Airbus A320			BA Regional	On Order
G-EUOI	Airbus A320			BA Regional	On Order
G-EUOJ	Airbus A320			BA Regional	On Order
G-EUOK	Airbus A320			BA Regional	On Order
G-EUOL	Airbus A320			BA Regional	On Order
G-EUOM	Airbus A320			BA Regional	On Order
G-EUON	Airbus A320			BA Regional	On Order
G-EUOO	Airbus A320			BA Regional	On Order
G-EUOP	Airbus A320			BA Regional	On Order
G-EUOR	Airbus A320			BA Regional	On Order
G-EUOS	Airbus A320			BA Regional	On Order
G-EUOT	Airbus A320			BA Regional	On Order
G-EUOU	Airbus A320			BA Regional	On Order
G-EUOV	Airbus A320			BA Regional	Order Option
G-EUOW	Airbus A320			BA Regional	Order Option
G-EUOX	Airbus A320			BA Regional	Order Option
G-EUOY	Airbus A320			BA Regional	Order Option
G-EUOZ	Airbus A320			BA Regional	Order Option
G-EUPA	Airbus A319-131	Union Flag		BA Regional BHX	
G-EUPB	Airbus A319-131	Union Flag		BA Regional BHX	
G-EUPC	Airbus A319-131	Union Flag		BA Regional BHX	
G-EUPD	Airbus A319-131	Union Flag		BA Regional BHX	
G-EUPE	Airbus A319-131	Union Flag		BA Regional BHX	
G-EUPF	Airbus A319-131	Union Flag		BA Regional BHX	
G-EUPG	Airbus A319-131	Union Flag		BA Regional BHX	
G-EUPH	Airbus A319-131	Union Flag		BA Regional BHX	Del 04/00
G-EUPI	Airbus A319-131	Union Flag		BA Regional BHX	Del 05/00
G-EUPJ	Airbus A319-131	Union Flag		BA Regional	Del 05/00
G-EUPK	Airbus A319-131	Union Flag		BA Regional	Del 05/00
G-EUPL	Airbus A319-131	Union Flag		BA Regional	Del 06/00
G-EUPM	Airbus A319-131	Union Flag		BA Regional	Del 07/00
G-EUPN	Airbus A319-131	Union Flag		BA Regional	Del 07/00
G-EUPO	Airbus A319-131	Union Flag		BA Regional	Del 08/00
G-EUPP	Airbus A319-131	Union Flag		BA Regional	Del 11/01
G-EUPR	Airbus A319-131	Union Flag		BA Regional	Del 11/01

Reg	Type	Colours	Name	Fleet	Notes
G-EUPS	Airbus A319-131			BA Regional	Del 2001
G-EUPT	Airbus A319-131			BA Regional	Del 2001
G-EUPU	Airbus A319-131			BA Regional	Del 2001
G-EUPV	Airbus A319-131			BA Regional	Del 2001
G-EUPW	Airbus A319-131			BA Regional	Del 2001
G-EUPX	Airbus A319-131			BA Regional	Del 2001
G-EUPY	Airbus A319-131			BA Regional	Del 2001
G-EUPZ	Airbus A319-131			BA Regional	Del 2001
G-GBTA	Boeing 737-436	Youm-Al-Suq	*County of Middlesex*	BA (Euro LGW)	
G-GBTB	Boeing 737-436			BA (Euro LGW)	Leased from IFLC
G-GFFA	Boeing737-500	Union Flag	-	BA Regional	Del 04/00
G-GFFB	Boeing737-500	Union Flag	-	BA Regional	Del 04/00
G-GFFC	Boeing737-500	Union Flag	-	BA Regional	Del 04/00
G-GFFD	Boeing737-500	Union Flag	-	BA Regional	Del 04/00
G-GFFE	Boeing737-500	Union Flag	-	BA Regional	Del 04/00
G-GFFF	Boeing737-500	Union Flag	-	BA Regional	Del 04/00
G-GFFG	Boeing737-500	Union Flag	-	BA Regional	Del 04/00
G-GFFH	Boeing737-500	Union Flag	-	BA Regional	Del 04/00
G-GFFI	Boeing737-500	Union Flag	-	BA Regional	Del 04/00
G-GFFJ	Boeing737-500	Union Flag	-	BA Regional	Del 04/00
G-GNTE	Saab 340	Benyhone Tartan		Business Air (Br Regional)	
G-IGOA	Boeing 737-3YO	Cyan	*go again/let's go*	Go Fly Ltd	
G-IGOC	Boeing 737-3YO	Purple	*go today/just go*	Go Fly Ltd	
G-IGOE	Boeing 737-3YO	Magenta	*go together/ready to go*	Go Fly Ltd	
G-IGOF	Boeing 737-3Q8	Lime Green	*go now/all go*	Go Fly Ltd	
G-IGOG	Boeing 737-3YO	Red	*go often/come and go*	Go Fly Ltd	
G-IGOH	Boeing 737-3YO	Mustard	*go for it/don't wait go*	Go Fly Ltd	
G-IGOI	Boeing 737-33A	Yellow	*go enjoy/away we go*	Go Fly Ltd	
G-IGOJ	Boeing 737-36N	Purple	*go anytime/free to go*	Go Fly Ltd	
G-IGOK	Boeing 737-36N	Navy Blue	*get set go/go as you are*	Go Fly Ltd	
G-IGOL	Boeing 737-36N	Terracotta	*go exploring/love to go*	Go Fly Ltd	
G-IGOM	Boeing 737-36N	Purple	*go for a break/off we go*	Go Fly Ltd	
G-IGOP	Boeing 737-36N	Pink	*go ahead/away we go*	Go Fly Ltd	
G-IGOR	Boeing 737-36N	Turquoise	*go to work/off you go*	Go Fly Ltd	
G-ISLE	Short 360			Br Regional Airlines	
G-LGNA	Saab 340	Benyhone Tartan		Loganair	
G-LGNB	Saab 340	Waves of the City		Loganair	
G-LGNC	Saab 340	Union Flag	-	Loganair	
G-MABR	BAe.146-100	Union Flag	-	British Regional	
G-MAJA	BAe Jetstream 41			Br Regional Airlines	
G-MAJB	BAe Jetstream 41	Ndebele Martha		Br Regional Airlines	
G-MAJC	BAe Jetstream 41	Colum (Celtic)		Br Regional Airlines	
G-MAJD	BAe Jetstream 41			Br Regional Airlines	
G-MAJE	BAe Jetstream 41			Br Regional Airlines	
G-MAJF	BAe Jetstream 41			Br Regional Airlines	
G-MAJG	BAe Jetstream 41			Br Regional Airlines	
G-MAJH	BAe Jetstream 41		*Viscount Tonypandy*	Br Regional Airlines	
G-MAJI	BAe Jetstream 41			Br Regional Airlines	
G-MAJJ	BAe Jetstream 41		*Lord Louis Mountbatten*	Br Regional Airlines	
G-MAJK	BAe Jetstream 41	Wings		Br Regional Airlines	
G-MAJL	BAe Jetstream 41	Chelsea Rose	*R. J. Mitchell*	Br Regional Airlines	
G-MAJM	BAe Jetstream 41			Br Regional Airlines	
G-MANE	BAe ATP			Br Regional Airlines	
G-MANF	BAe ATP			Br Regional Airlines	
G-MANG	BAe ATP			Br Regional Airlines	
G-MANH	BAe ATP			Br Regional Airlines	
G-MANJ	BAe ATP			Br Regional Airlines	
G-MANL	BAe ATP			Br Regional Airlines	
G-MANM	BAe ATP		*Elaine Griffiths*	Br Regional Airlines	
G-MANO	BAe ATP	Rendezvous		Br Regional Airlines	
G-MANP	BAe ATP			Br Regional Airlines	
G-MANS	BAe146-200A			Br Regional Airlines	

Reg	Type	Colours	Name	Fleet	Notes
G-MAUD	BAe ATP	Blue Poole		Br Regional Airlines	
G-MEDA	Airbus A320	Whale Rider		British Mediterranean Airlines	
G-MEDB	Airbus A320	Rendezvous		British Mediterranean Airlines	
G-MEDD	Airbus A320	Crossing Borders		British Mediterranean Airlines	
G-MEDE	Airbus A320	Union Flag		British Mediterranean Airlines	
G-MSKA	Boeing 737-500	Union Flag		Maersk UK	
G-MSKB	Boeing 737-500	Union Flag		Maersk UK	
G-MSKC	Boeing 737-500	Union Flag		Maersk UK	
G-MSKD	Boeing 737-500	Whale Rider		Maersk UK	
G-MSKE	Boeing 737-500	Delftblue Daybreak		Maersk UK	
G-MSKJ	BAe Jetstream 41	Ndebele Martha		Maersk UK	For disposal
G-MSKK	Canadair RJ 200LR	Wings		Maersk UK	
G-MSKL	Canadair RJ 200LR	Ndebele Emmly		Maersk UK	
G-MSKM	Canadair RJ 200LR	Bauhaus		Maersk UK	
G-MSKN	Canadair RJ 200LR	Chelsea Rose		Maersk UK	
G-MSKO	Canadair RJ 200LR	Crossing Borders		Maersk UK	
G-MSKP	Canadair RJ 200LR	Union Flag		Maersk UK	
G-MSKR	Canadair RJ 200LR	Union Flag		Maersk UK	Due 02/2000
G-MSKS	Canadair RJ 200LR	Union Flag		Maersk UK	Due 04/2000
G-MSKT	Canadair RJ 200LR			Maersk UK	Del 10/00
G-MSKU	Canadair RJ 200LR			Maersk UK	Del 11/00
G-NJIA	BAe146	Union Flag		National Jets Italia	
G-NJIB	BAe146	Union Flag		National Jets Italia	
G-NJIC	BAe146	Union Flag		National Jets Italia	
G-NJID	BAe146	Union Flag		National Jets Italia	
G-NJIE	BAe146	Union Flag		National Jets Italia	
G-NVSA	DHC Dash 8-311	All White		Brymon	
G-NVSB	DHC Dash 8-311	Delftblue Daybreak		Brymon	
G-NVSC	DHC Dash 8-311			Brymon	
G-OAMS	Boeing 737-37Q	Rendezvous		BA Regional BHX	
G-OBEA	BAe Jetstream 31			Maersk UK	
G-ODUS	Boeing 737-37Q	Waves & Cranes		BA Regional BHX	Leased
G-OFRA	Boeing 737-37Q	Bauhaus		BA Regional BHX	Leased
G-OGBA	Boeing 737-34S	Waves & Cranes	Mons Calpe (Gibraltar)	GB Airways	
G-OGBB	Boeing 737-34S	Colum (Celtic)	Mons Pico Ruivo (Madeira)	GB Airways	
G-OGBC	Boeing 737-34S	Koguty Lowickie	Mons Abyla (Morocco)	GB Airways	
G-OGBD	Boeing 737-3L9	Ndebele Martha	Mons Torellas (Mallorca)	GB Airways	
G-OGBE	Boeing 737-3L9	Crossing Borders	Mons Imdina (Malta)	GB Airways	
G-OHAJ	Boeing 737-37Q	Delftblue Daybreak		BA Regional BHX	Leased
G-OINV	BAe 146-300	Union Flag	-	British Regional	
G-OMUC	Boeing 737-37Q	Colum (Celtic)		BA Regional BHX	Leased
G-OSEA	BN-2B-26 Islander			Loganair	
G-RAES	Boeing 777-236 (IGW)	Delftblue Daybreak		BA	
G-TREN	Boeing 737-4S3	Blue Poole	Mons Estrala (Portugal)	GB Airways	
G-TTOA	Airbus A320			GB Airways	Del 05/00
G-UKTM	ATR 72	Union Flag		Br Regional Airlines	Leased
G-UKTN	ATR 72	Union Flag		Br Regional Airlines	Leased
G-VIIA	Boeing 777-236 (IGW)	Waves of the City		BA	
G-VIIB	Boeing 777-236 (IGW)			BA	
G-VIIC	Boeing 777-236 (IGW)			BA	
G-VIID	Boeing 777-236 (IGW)			BA	
G-VIIE	Boeing 777-236 (IGW)	Union Flag		BA	
G-VIIF	Boeing 777-236 (IGW)			BA	
G-VIIG	Boeing 777-236 (IGW)			BA	
G-VIIH	Boeing 777-236 (IGW)			BA	
G-VIII	Boeing 777-236 (IGW)			BA	
G-VIIJ	Boeing 777-236 (IGW)	Benyhone Tartan		BA	
G-VIIK	Boeing 777-236 (IGW)	Animals & Trees		BA	
G-VIIL	Boeing 777-236 (IGW)	Wings		BA	
G-VIIM	Boeing 777-236 (IGW)	Waves & Cranes		BA	
G-VIIN	Boeing 777-236 (IGW)	Whale Rider		BA	
G-VIIO	Boeing 777-236 (IGW)	Chelsea Rose		BA/AML (Gatwick)	
G-VIIP	Boeing 777-236 (IGW)	Colum (Celtic)		BA/AML (Gatwick)	

Reg	Type	Colours	Name	Fleet	Notes
G-VIIR	Boeing 777-236 (IGW)	Benyhone Tartan		BA/AML (Gatwick)	
G-VIIS	Boeing 777-236 (IGW)	Chelsea Rose		BA	
G-VIIT	Boeing 777-236 (IGW)	Rendezvous		BA	
G-VIIU	Boeing 777-236 (IGW)	Delftblue Daybreak		BA	
G-VIIV	Boeing 777-236 (IGW)	Union Flag		BA	
G-VIIW	Boeing 777-236 (IGW)	Union Flag		BA	
G-VIIX	Boeing 777-236 (IGW)	Union Flag		BA	
G-VIIY	Boeing 777-236 (IGW)	Union Flag		BA	
G-WACK	Shorts 360-100			Loganair	
G-XBHX	Boeing 737-37N	Grand Union		BA Regional BHX	Leased
G-XMAN	Boeing 737-37N	Golden Khokhloma		BA Regional BHX	Leased
G-YMMA	Boeing 777-236	Union Flag		BA	
G-YMMB	Boeing 777-236			BA	
G-YMMC	Boeing 777-236			BA	
G-YMMD	Boeing 777-236			BA	
G-YMME	Boeing 777-236			BA	Del 21/03/00
G-YMMF	Boeing 777-236			BA	Del 05/2000
G-YMMG	Boeing 777-236			BA	Del 12/2000
G-YMMH	Boeing 777-236			BA	Del 01/2001
G-YMMI	Boeing 777-236			BA	Del 02/2001
G-YMMJ	Boeing 777-236			BA	Del 02/2001
G-YMMK	Boeing 777-236			BA	Del 03/2001
G-YMML	Boeing 777-236			BA	Del 04/2001
G-YMMM	Boeing 777-236			BA	Del 05/2001
G-YMMN	Boeing 777-236			BA	Del 06/2001
G-YMMO	Boeing 777-236			BA	Del 09/2001
G-YMMP	Boeing 777-236			BA	Del 01/2002
G-ZZZA	Boeing 777-236		*Sir Frank Whittle*	BA	
G-ZZZB	Boeing 777-236		*Sir William Sefton Brancker*	BA	
G-ZZZC	Boeing 777-236	Rendezvous	*Charles Edward Kingsford Smith*	BA	
G-ZZZD	Boeing 777-236		*Orville Wright/Wilbur Wright*	BA	
G-ZZZE	Boeing 777-236		*Sir John Alcock/ Sir Arthur Whitten Brown*	BA	
N495MC	Boeing 747F	Chelsea Rose		BA Cargo World	Leased
OY-MUE	Jetstream 31	Union Flag		Sun Air of Scandinavia	
OY-SVF	BAe Jetstream 31	Waves of the City		Sun Air of Scandinavia	
OY-SVI	BAe ATP	Benyhone Tartan		Sun Air of Scandinavia	
OY-SVJ	BAe Jetstream 31	Blomsterang		Sun Air of Scandinavia	
OY-SVR	BAe Jetstream 31	Rendezvous		Sun Air of Scandinavia	For disposal
OY-SVS	BAe Jetstream 41	Ndebele		Sun Air of Scandinavia	
OY-SVT	BAe ATP	Colum (Celtic)		Sun Air of Scandinavia	
OY-SVU	BAe ATP	Wings		Sun Air of Scandinavia	
OY-SVW	BAe Jetstream 41	Wings	*Port of Arhus*	Sun Air of Scandinavia	
OY-SVZ	BAe Jetstream 31			Sun Air of Scandinavia	
PH-BRL	Embraer EMB-120RT			BASE Airlines	
PH-BRM	Embraer EMB-120RT			BASE Airlines	
PH-BRP	Embraer EMB-120RT	Union Flag		BASE Airlines	
PH-KJB	BAe Jetstream 31			BASE Airlines	
PH-KJG	BAe Jetstream 31	Delftblue Daybreak		BASE Airlines	
ZS-NLN	Boeing 737-236	Waves & Cranes		Comair (S Africa)	
ZS-NNG	Boeing 737-236	Bauhaus		Comair (S Africa)	
ZS-NNH	Boeing 737-236	Blue Poole		Comair (S Africa)	
ZS-NOU	Boeing 727-230	Blomsterang		Comair (S Africa)	
ZS-NOV	Boeing 727-230	Delftblue Daybreak		Comair (S Africa)	
ZS-NVR	Boeing 727	Waves of the City		Comair (S Africa)	
ZS-NZV	Boeing 727-230	Colum (Celtic)		Comair (S Africa)	
ZS-OBO	Boeing 727	Benyhone Tartan		Comair (S Africa)	
ZS-OLA	Boeing 737-236	Water Dreaming		Comair (S Africa)	Ex G-BKYE
ZS-OLB	Boeing 737-236	Union Flag		Comair (S Africa)	Ex G-BKYI
ZS-SBN	Boeing 737-244	Ndebele Martha		Comair (S Africa)	
ZS-SBO	Boeing 737-244	Koguty Lowickie		Comair (S Africa)	
ZS-SBR	Boeing 737-244	Animals & Trees		Comair (S Africa)	

5. The Product

Passenger Services

Although it is tempting to regard British Airways as the operator of a high-quality fleet of modern aircraft, interest in the technical aspects of the air transport business should not obscure the fact that all airlines exist to carry passengers and the most successful airlines are those that succeed in persuading the maximum number of people to fly with them rather than with a competitor. In the past, most national airlines could count on a captive market from within their own country and there was little advantage to be gained by the passenger in flying with other airlines as there was almost no competition on fares. However, the continuing deregulation of air transport in recent years, together with the enormous productivity of modern jet airliners, has led to aggressive campaigns by all carriers to increase their share of the market. In these circumstances it is not enough simply to offer flights between various points and publish a scale of fares. The customer almost invariably has a choice of airlines when planning a journey and will consider a whole range of factors before making a decision. Many of these will be purely technical in nature such as the type and age of the aircraft, and the airline's safety reputation. However, the potential traveller will also consider the fare to be paid, the facilities offered at the departure and arrival airport, the seating arrangement on the aircraft, and the standard and nature of the in-flight catering and service.

People travel for many reasons but in general they fall into one of two categories: business and leisure. For those in the latter category, price is usually an important factor, while the business traveller will often be prepared to pay more in return for better service and greater comfort. These are, of course, sweeping generalisations and each potential passenger will have differing requirements. British Airways has built much of its success on a well-deserved reputation for offering excellent service to all categories of passenger and has continually striven to ensure that its standards compare with, and often exceed, those of its competitors. In a highly competitive situation, British Airways has refined the marketing of its various levels of service to the point where each offers clearly definable attributes which can be sold to the potential customer as providing better value than those of other airlines. Traditionally, most airlines have offered three classes of service — First, Business and Economy — although these are usually applied only to long-haul flights. Most other international and some domestic flights have only Business and Economy, while a single class is generally acceptable for short-duration domestic flights. British Airways generally follows this pattern but has established significant variations within each and has devised other unique products which are all known by a distinctive brand name. These are constantly reviewed and updated in the light of experience, competition from other airlines and passenger reaction.

Concorde

The supersonic fleet is operated as a separate division for commercial as well as technical purposes and Concorde is marketed as a unique brand of travel — offering both speed and elegance in one high-profile package which can be matched by only one other airline. Concorde passengers pay premium fares (over £6,000 for a transatlantic return flight) for the experience and consequently receive the highest standards of service from British Airways. As time saving is one of the main reasons for choosing Concorde, great efforts have been made to ensure that the hours saved in the air are not wasted on the ground. Check-in times, at dedicated desks reserved for supersonic passengers, can be left as late as 30min prior to departure and the aircraft is subsequently boarded directly from exclusive Concorde lounges which offer every comfort and facility. This includes the new Concorde Room, designed by Sir Terence Conran, at New York's Kennedy Airport. Passengers with hand baggage may check in by telephone and all can use the dedicated Fast Track channel to reduce the time spent on non-airline airport formalities. At Heathrow's Terminal 4, British Airways has opened a Lounge Pavilion which incorporates facilities for both Concorde and First Class

incorporating a visitor's seat so that two people can conduct business or dine together as they wish. All of these seats convert, at the touch of a button, to a full-length 6ft 6in (198cm) flat bed and a personal video and entertainment centre is naturally incorporated. A delicious *à la carte* dining menu can be enjoyed at any stage of the flight and for those passengers who do not wish their rest to be disturbed, a similar meal can be served prior to take-off at the airport and a sleeper suit and duvet cover are provided to ensure a good night's rest once aboard the aircraft. At Heathrow and Gatwick dedicated First Class lounges are available in the Pavilions and these can also be used to freshen up after arrival. In addition, First Class passengers have access to over 180 lounges worldwide and receive priority transfers, if required, between Terminals 1 and 4 at Heathrow. First Class is available on all British Airways intercontinental flights which are operated mainly by Boeing 747s where the accommodation is in the nose cabin on the maindeck, or by the new Boeing 777 which has 14 or 17 sleeper seats in the forward part of the passenger cabin. The new First Class seating is not available on the Boeing 767 which offers only Club Class accommodation.

passengers. On arrival, a high priority is accorded to baggage delivery; at New York, the journey to Manhattan can be completed by helicopter if required at no extra cost, and a dedicated American Eagle flight operates to and from Washington National airport. On the aircraft, the cabin has been specially designed to offer a calm and restful environment and all aircraft are regularly refurbished. The catering is of the highest standard possible with many dishes created specially for British Airways by famous international chefs. Additional cabin staff are carried to ensure the very best of service. The normal schedule leaves London at 10.30am and arrives in New York at 9.20am (New York time). Baggage is delivered within 8min of arrival.

First Class

While other airlines have thought it necessary to give their best level of service rather confusing names such as Royal, Presidential and Upper, British Airways has stayed with the title which has a traditional and unambiguous meaning — First Class. The current product and service features date from 1996 when the airline's First Class service was completely overhauled and some completely new concepts introduced, including a specially commissioned seating system which by means of subtle screening gives the impression of a private cabin. Single or double seats are available, the former

Club World

This is the title of British Airways' business class brand on intercontinental flights and even as this book went to press early in 2000 a substantial and spectacular improvement to the facilities on offer was announced, replacing the last major upgrade dating from 1996. In line with British Airways' policy of concentrating on premium and business class passengers, it has come up with its unique 'lounge in the sky' concept. The individual seats echo the general design of the First Class seats in the form of a comfortable armchair with a built-in foot rest, and convert easily into a fully flat six-foot bed. There is a full audio and video entertainment system and provision for workaholics to plug in

Left: **First Class offers unrivalled accommodation and a choice of excellent meals.**
British Airways

their laptop computers, as well as a built-in personal telephone. However, the most striking feature of the Club World cabins is that the seating is no longer arranged in orderly forward-facing rows, but cleverly arranged in groups of alternate forward and rearward facing seats offering a considerable amount of personal space — up by 30% on conventional layouts — while still retaining a degree of privacy. The result is impressive and different and is based on extensive research of passenger preferences and requirements. The new cabin will gradually replace the previous 2-3-2 seating configuration set at a 50-inch pitch aboard 747s, 767s and 777s during the course of the year. Apart from changes to the cabin environment, the emphasis remains on making life as relaxed as possible for the business traveller and there are exclusive check-in desks and separate lounges offering business facilities. At Heathrow there is car parking service which allows the passenger to drive up to the terminal and hand the car over to an attendant who will see to its parking. Catering is of a high standard, featuring a five-course meal with a choice of menus, and a new feature called 'Raid the Larder' allows passengers to help themselves to snacks and other treats after the main meal has been served. As an alternative, pre-flight dining is available for some UK services from the US East Coast which allows the maximum amount of sleep on the relatively short overnight flight. On arrival there is a priority delivery of baggage, assisted at London Gatwick and Heathrow by access to a fast track arrivals channel allowing a speedy

passage through airport controls, as well as the welcome facility of arrivals lounges.

Club Europe

As the name implies, this is the Club Class level of service as applied to the European route network where many business travellers are regular customers, often making return flights in the same day. With this in mind, flights are arranged to facilitate business requirements and passengers can check-in for their return flight on departure, thus saving time and hassle at the end of the day. British Airways offers Club Europe service on some 350 flights a day to 60 destinations. Naturally there are separate desks and access to the Club Europe lounge in Terminal 4 at Heathrow. This can seat up to 400 and is comprehensively equipped with desks, phones and fax machines as well as having access to a spa facility where travellers can change and have a shower. British Airways Club Class passengers benefit from access to 30 similar lounges at other European airports. Also available is the express car parking service and priority baggage handling. The airline's short-haul aircraft do not have separate Club cabins but Club Europe passengers are allocated seats at the forward part of the aircraft which, in flight, is curtained off by a movable divider and this allows considerable flexibility in booking and ticketing. Normally the centre seat in each row of three is left vacant to give passengers more space and the seating is set at a 34-inch pitch although as part of the improvement to premium services new permanent leather seats are being installed in

Club World cabin areas. A high standard of catering is offered and there is usually a choice of main courses. British Airways claims that there are no less than 10 different ways of checking-in including telephone check-in from 15.00 hrs on the day before departure to self-service machines which can be used up to 20 minutes before departure in some cases.

World Traveller Plus

A new brand introduced early in 2000 which offers up to five rows of a new seat in a separate cabin area. These seats are wider than the standard economy seat and have a built-in personal telephone as well as a power supply for laptop computers. However, the most significant feature of World Traveller Plus is the increased seat pitch which now stands at 38 inches, up to 7 inches more than the standard World Traveller seating. Apart from the seating improvements, the service otherwise corresponds to that described in the next section.

New World Traveller, Euro Traveller

These are the names applied to British Airways' basic level of service on long and short-haul international flights and were first introduced in 1991 as part of a general improvement to the Economy Class. Despite being the least expensive class, high standards of service and catering are maintained and little touches such as newspapers, fruit juices, hot towels and comfort packs, as well as a complimentary bar service help to relax the passenger. World Traveller cabins feature an in-flight television and audio entertainment system, while Euro Travellers are provided with an audio system. Seating pitch is 32in, less than Club but still adequate and greater than that offered by many rival airlines. With the introduction of the Boeing 777, British Airways has upgraded the product under the name New World Traveller and this offers more comfortable seats with lumbar support and adjustable head rests and foot rests. These incorporate seatback video screens with 12 entertainment channels, while there is also a four-channel audio system. A popular innovation is the ability to reserve specific seats at the time of booking. The New

World Traveller brand will also be applied to the Boeing 747 fleet, with all aircraft scheduled to be fitted out by April 2001.

Super Shuttle

The intensive high-frequency shuttle operations serving Manchester, Glasgow, Belfast and Edinburgh from Heathrow have their own special brand of service and facilities for passengers. Originally started in 1983, it has been continuously improved over the years and now carries over 3.5 million passengers a year. The emphasis is on convenience of use together with guaranteed seats, although there are now alternative fare structures for business and leisure travellers. The former is called Super Shuttle Executive and retains fully flexible ticketing and the turn-up-and-take-off guarantee which is the concept's hallmark, while leisure travellers can take advantage of Super Shuttle Savers which offer low fares but with less flexibility. A popular innovation has been the introduction of automated ticketing machines which can be accessed using British Airways' own credit cards. In-flight there is a one-class service with hot meals at appropriate times of the day, except on the Manchester run where cold meals are served due to the short flight time.

Executive Club

Membership of the British Airways Executive Club offers substantial benefits, particularly to business travellers who fly regularly. There are three levels of membership (Blue, Silver and Gold) but all offer priority seat allocation on busy flights, dedicated reservation and service centres and worldwide discount rates on hotels, car hire and travel insurance. Gold and Silver members have access to Executive lounges at many airports.

The prospective passenger will often look to an airline to provide more than just the flight, no matter how pleasant it may be, and so all operators have connections in other aspects of the travel business including car rental, hotels and holidays. British Airways is no exception and has marketing agreements with such concerns around the world. In addition, it owns British Airways Holidays, Air Miles Travel Promotions Ltd and Travel Automation Services

Ltd, the latter better known as the Galileo computer reservations system, while it also owns a small stake in Hogg Robinson, a travel agency chain specialising in business travel arrangements.

Catering

British Airways places great stress on the quality of its cabin service and an integral part of this is the provision of in-flight meals. These can vary from a simple coffee and biscuits to the elaborate multi-course menus offered to First Class passengers. Apart from being interesting and pleasant to eat, each meal must meet exacting technical standards covering presentation, taste, storage and hygiene as well as meeting dietary, ethnic and religious requirements of a wide cross-section of travellers. Little wonder then that catering is given a high priority within British Airways which takes great pride in the results. The investment involved is exemplified by the 180,000sq ft European Catering Centre at Heathrow which became fully operational in January 1992 and provides up to 29,000 meals a day for short-haul services operating out of London. Other establishments cover the long-haul operation where more than one meal is served on each flight and there are extensive contractual arrangements with other airlines and catering organisations to provide meals to British Airways' specifications at overseas departure points. The airline recently carried out a complex exercise to compare the costs and quality of its in-house organisation with products bought in from contract caterers, resulting in a significant improvement in the performance of its own unit.

Cabin Crews

To the average passenger the face of British Airways is represented by the steward or stewardess who looks after them during a flight. The airline employs 14,864 cabin staff in its Mainline fleet alone. These are all trained at the Heathrow Cabin Services Training Centre where, in addition to learning how to look after passengers and their requirements, they are also taught the vital procedures to be used in the event of any emergency situation such as a fire or a ditching. They are also taught the correct use and operation of safety-related equipment such as emergency exits, escape slides and lifejackets as well as basic first-aid procedures.

Out of the total number of cabin staff, over 700 are recruited from overseas and are assigned to various long-haul flights in order to provide a point of reference for passengers from abroad who may not speak English and whose culture may require a slightly amended type of service. Out of these 700, approximately 120 are Portuguese or Spanish speakers for the South American routes, another 150 are Japanese and a further 100 are Chinese, based at Hong Kong. On a typical 747 flight there will be a cabin crew of 15, of whom four or five may be overseas staff. On the long-haul 767s there are usually two overseas staff out of a complement of nine. Additional Hispanic staff cover direct services to Mexico and cater for the increasing numbers of Spanish-speaking passengers on flights to and from the southern United States.

British Airways World Cargo

Unusually for a major airline, British Airways operates no dedicated cargo aircraft and almost all freight is carried in the underfloor holds of aircraft on regular scheduled services, although the Boeing 747 fleet does include three Combi variants which can also carry freight on a section of the maindeck. Despite this, the airline carried 815,873 tonnes of freight in the operating year 1998, a 13% improvement on the previous year. It is also the highest figure of any airline not operating specialist cargo aircraft, and is eighth overall in terms of freight tonne kilometres and freight tonnes carried according to IATA figures. When it is considered that a 747-400 can carry up 20 tonnes of cargo in addition to its passenger load, it can be understood where the capacity comes from. A 767 carries 12.3 or 11 tonnes depending on configuration and the 757 on scheduled services carries up to 5.8 tonnes. Occasionally, the airline will lease additional capacity or part purchase capacity on other specialist freight services. In addition, British Airways maintains four European road haulage hubs which feed cargo from the Continent into the Heathrow and Gatwick-based intercontinental

Right: **Adjacent to the new World Cargo Centre is a separate facility for handling perishable goods such as flowers and vegetables which require a fast turnround.** *Adrian Meredith Photography via British Airways*

services. The first of these was established at Maastricht in 1986 and others are at Helsingborg in Sweden and Lyon, France.

Since October 1992, the airline's freight and cargo business has been organised under the title British Airways World Cargo. It is run as a separate profit centre responsible for its own strategic planning, marketing, budgeting and financial affairs, and was the first British Airways department to be accorded this status. Although a significant proportion of the cargo is carried on scheduled passenger flights, there is one pure freight aircraft which can be seen in British Airways colours. This is a Boeing 747-400F on a five-year lease from Atlas. However, BA also has capacity-sharing agreements with Singapore Airlines, Japan Airlines and Korean Airlines, all of which also use 747s, as well as EVA Air which flies the MD-11F. At other times, British Airways has entered into short-term contracts with various specialist cargo operators such as MK Airlines, DAS Air Cargo and Cargo Lion, all of which fly DC-8s, and also with UK-based operators such as Channel Express which now flies converted Airbus A300s.

Of the world network total of over 800,000 tonnes of freight in 1998, no less than 550,000 tonnes passed through London's Heathrow airport and of this some 60% was in transit. This creates a cargo handling problem on a massive scale, particularly as the transit cargo will have to be off-loaded, broken down into part loads and reassembled into other units before being reloaded on to another aircraft and flown out. To cater for this demand, and to improve efficiency and speed of cargo handling, British

Airways announced in 1996 that it would build a new World Cargo complex at Heathrow. This was completed in 1999 and its creation was Europe's largest construction project, while its price tag of £250 million represented British Airways' largest ever non-aircraft investment. In terms of size it is quite staggering. With a length of 300m, a width of 95m and a height of 37m, it is claimed that it would hold 6,000 London double-decker buses (or, more prosaically, four Boeing 747s). Some 1,100 staff work here using sophisticated cargo manipulators, each costing £200,000, to move the cargo around and build up aircraft-sized loads. A sophisticated tracking system using electronic barcode readers keeps track of every item of cargo, no matter how large or small. As it stands, the World Cargo Centre can handle up to 800,000 tonnes per annum, and this can be increased to 1 million tonnes with a modest expansion of the facility. The previous Freight Centre International is being converted at a cost of £2.5 million to become a Special Handling Centre which will cater for the courier and premium express market as well as specialist loads such as livestock. To handle perishable goods such as flowers, fruit and vegetables, a new 70,000sq ft centre is being built to replace the existing smaller facility. Surprisingly, this market accounts for no less than 17% of World Cargo's total revenue. Although most of British Airways' World Cargo operation is based around the main cargo freight terminals at Heathrow and Gatwick, there is also a major cargo facility at Manchester, opened in 1986 at a cost of £7 million.

6. Support Services

Left: **There are literally hundreds of miles of wiring to be checked during a major inspection on a Boeing 747.**
British Airways Engineering

Although it is easy to think of British Airways just as a fleet of aircraft carrying passengers and cargo around the world, it must be remembered that this could not happen without the support of thousands of people on the ground carrying out a great variety of tasks including passenger handling, administration, training, engineering, transport, marketing, scheduling and a thousand and one other tasks which are vital to any airline. Some of these are briefly described below.

British Airways Engineering

In 1999 the British Airways fleet consisted of over 250 aircraft, ranging from the Boeing 737 to the supersonic Concorde and the high-technology Boeing 747-400, powered by a total of over 850 engines (excluding spares). Each aircraft is equipped with a variety of complex electrical, hydraulic and pneumatic systems as well as increasingly sophisticated avionics including navigation and communications equipment. To keep these aircraft flying reliably and safely British Airways has a maintenance and overhaul workforce of 8,628 staff, or just over 15% of total staff numbers. This is actually a reduction of over 1,000 on the figure three years ago when engineering accounted for some 20% of British Airways staff. The Engineering Division also earns a valuable

income through the overhaul of aircraft belonging to other airlines such as Canadian Airlines International, Continental Airlines, QANTAS, Air New Zealand and Cathay Pacific. Indeed, such is the size and complexity of the engineering task that in April 1995 British Airways Engineering became an operating division and profit centre run as a separate business within the British Airways Group and has its own Board of Directors and marketing department. Its turnover in the first five years was predicted to reach £1,000 million.

Once established in its new format, British Airways Engineering set in place a major reorganisation of its staff and facilities in order to improve efficiency, reduce costs and attract new business. This involved the establishment of three 'Fleet Streams', each dedicated to supporting specific aircraft types. Fleets 1 and 2 utilise the massive engineering base occupying a 220-acre site at Hatton Cross on the eastern edge of Heathrow where the former BEA and BOAC facilities were established during the early 1950s. Since then, new hangars, workshops, stores and offices have been added to make it one of the largest complexes of its type in the world. Fleet 1 looks after the Airbus A320, Boeing 757 and Boeing 767 fleets, while Fleet 2 is concerned with Boeing 747, Boeing 777 and Concorde fleets. At Gatwick, Fleet 3 looks after the entire Boeing 737 fleet, including both 200 and 400 series aircraft. All three fleets already provide maintenance facilities for third-party airlines at the various bases and British Airways Engineering is now actively marketing its skills, facilities and expertise to significantly increase such business.

In addition to the three Fleet Streams at Heathrow and Gatwick, British Airways Engineering also opened a major complex at Cardiff Airport in April 1993 which is dedicated solely to the overhaul and maintenance of the airline's fleet of Boeing 747s of all variants. Originally known as Project Dragonfly (an oblique reference to the Welsh location), this 70-acre development employs around 850 staff and now operates under the title of British Airways Maintenance Cardiff (BAMC). The purpose-built facility can accommodate three 747s simultaneously and every major check and modification can be carried out here. In the three years since starting operations, BAMC turned round some 120 aircraft including some from airlines such as Canadian Airlines International, Southern Air Transport, Evergreen, American International Airlines, Corsair and Tower Air as well as British Airways' own aircraft. In 1999 it also started the servicing of new Boeing 777s in direct competition with BA Engineering at Heathrow.

Wales is also the home of another British Airways Engineering subsidiary, British Airways Avionic Engineering Ltd (BAAE), which is based at a purpose-built 13,000sq m facility situated near Llantrisant, Mid-Glamorgan. Also opened in 1993, this organisation actively markets its expertise to other operators as well as taking care of British Airways' own requirements. The spread of work carried out is quite amazing and includes servicing and repairing a vast range of avionic equipment from radio and radar, through air data computers and navigation equipment to the increasingly sophisticated in-flight entertainment and communication facilities now finding their way into modern airliners.

Until December 1991 British Airways maintained a comprehensive engine overhaul facility, again in Wales, but this was sold to the American company General Electric which continues to carry out work for the airline under contract. Situated at Nantgarw, it replaced the previous facility at nearby Treforest and the complete range of British Airways engines is overhauled here.

To give some idea of the work involved in maintaining a modern airliner, the following inspection and maintenance schedule for a long-haul Boeing 747-400 provides a fascinating insight. Basically, it is organised into a series of increasingly complex checks as the aircraft passes various milestones based on accumulated flying hours. The following table also gives an indication of the manpower requirements at each stage.

Transit Check. Before every flight. Two engineers and a flight crew member.
Exterior check of the aircraft and engines for damage or leakage. Specific checks on listed items such as brake and tyre wear.

Ramp 1 Check. Daily. Four engineers.
Transit check plus additional checks on engine oil levels, tyre pressures, aircraft external lighting, cabin emergency equipment, engine health monitoring systems and assessment of technical log entries.

Ramp 2 Check. Every 190 flying hours. Four engineers.
Transit and Ramp 1 checks plus checks on APU and component oil levels, engine component oil levels, cabin interior condition and windows.

Ramp 3 Check. Every 540 flying hours. Six engineers.
Transit, Ramp 1 and 2 checks plus replacement of hydraulic systems filters, checks on cockpit and cabin seats and attachments, sterilisation of water system and detailed inspection of system filters. More detailed inspections on items covered in previous checks including avionic systems and standby power systems. Batteries changed.

Service Check 1. Every 1,060 flying hours during overnight stopovers at a maintenance base. 50 engineers.
All previous checks plus partial stripdown of structure and engines for detailed inspection. Replacement of worn components and soiled or

damaged cabin equipment and furnishings. Servicing of undercarriage struts. Total service check takes around two shifts (approximately 16hr) to complete.

Service Check 2. Every 2,120 flying hours. 50 engineers.
All above checks plus additional and more detailed inspections of specific areas. External wash of aircraft, system clarification function checks and deep cleaning of cabin water and waste systems. Requires three shifts to complete.

Service Check 3. Every 3,875 flying hours. 50 engineers.
All the above plus detailed inspection of flying controls, structure and engines. Fluid levels drained and refilled in major mechanical components. Aircraft washed, avionics systems integrated checks. Cabin condition assessed and repaired in depth. Requires four shifts.

Inter Check 1. Every 6,360 flying hours. 160 engineers.
Detailed inspection and repair of aircraft, engines, components, systems and cabin, including operating mechanisms, flight controls, structural tolerances. Takes between seven and eight days.

Inter Check 2. Every 12,720 flying hours. 160 engineers.
All the above plus additional system function checks. Takes eight to nine days.

Major service. Every 24,000 flying hours or every five years if sooner. 180 engineers.
A very intensive inspection taking between 20 and 25 days. Involves major structural inspections including attention to fatigue corrosion. The aircraft is virtually dismantled, repaired and rebuilt as required, with systems and parts tested and repaired or replaced as necessary. Corrosion prevention and control tasks carried out.

Right: **British Airways carries the world on its shoulders: the bronze statue outside the Compass Centre.** *Author*

Training and Administration

Simulator Centre (Cranebank)

British Airways has a fleet of over 200 aircraft which carry passengers all over the world but it also owns another fleet which is in constant operation, can fly anywhere and do anything, but which never carries a single passenger and never leaves the ground. This is, of course, the 17-strong fleet of aircraft simulators housed in the British Airways Cranebank Centre on the eastern side of Heathrow. These amazing electronic devices are realistic reproductions of the flightdeck of a specific aircraft and in most cases they have a six-axis motion system to give absolute realism during the course of simulated flights. In addition, the more modern simulators are fitted with advanced computer-generated visual systems which give a realistic wide-angled view over areas of terrain and airports for use when simulating landings and take-offs.

The fleet at Cranebank includes modern simulators for the newest aircraft types such as the 737-400, the 747-400 (4), the 767-300, and

the 777-200. In addition, there is also a 757 simulator as well as a another dual-purpose 757/767 example. There are also a number of simulators for older types such as the early versions of the 747 (100 and 200 series), the 737-200, and the BAC111S . These are mostly utilised by other airlines which still fly these aircraft. The Concorde simulator is at Filton in Bristol.

Waterside

Ever since the airline's formation in 1974, British Airways' administration has been carried out from a variety of centres scattered around the Heathrow perimeter. As the airport grew, it became increasingly congested and office space and staff facilities were increasingly difficult to locate. In 1993 the decision was taken to develop a new purpose-built corporate business centre on reclaimed land at Harmondsworth, just to the northwest of Heathrow. Officially opened at the end of 1997, it now accommodates some 2,800 staff and is set in 240 acres of carefully landscaped grounds. It was designed by the Norwegian architect Niels Torp using a village concept of streets and neighbourhoods. It consist of six interconnected four-storey buildings and offers a light and airy open-plan working environment. Apart from work facilities, it also includes shops, restaurants, a hairdressing salon, a fitness suite and gym as well as a medical centre and conference/training centre. The total cost was £200 million but British Airways now has a corporate centre befitting its status as one of the world's greatest airlines.

Compass Centre

Yet another major property investment by British Airways, this was completed in November 1993 to house the airline's planning and support activities for its 18,000 flight and cabin crew. Sited on the north side of Heathrow, the building's striking external façade is designed to reduce reflections from the airport's radar equipment and therefore prevent unwanted interference on air traffic control radar screens. The main departments at the Compass Centre are Flight Operations, Cabin Services and Operations. The latter is the organisation which maintains a 24hr watch on the airline's aircraft

operations and is responsible for allocating aircraft to fly the published flight schedule. It is also responsible for organising the response to any service disruptions which may be caused by a variety of factors such as weather, airport closures, airspace and airport congestion, and industrial action. In addition, it is responsible for preparing contingency plans to deal with various emergency scenarios. Flight Operations and Cabin Services are jointly responsible for ensuring that the correct number of correctly qualified flight and cabin crews are available for every BA flight worldwide — an extremely complex task in its own right. For services departing from Heathrow, there is a crew check-in facility where cabin crews can assemble while the pilots carry out the necessary pre-flight planning before linking up and travelling directly to the aircraft by coach.

Although, as already explained, the engineering facilities are situated in other locations, the Compass Centre does house the BA Engineering Central Control Unit. This is in direct touch with the Operations Centre and is therefore in a position to ensure that any engineering problem is immediately highlighted and the appropriate response planned to deal with it as soon as the aircraft arrives.

A final unit housed in the Compass Centre and one which, hopefully, is little utilised, is the Crisis Centre. This is split into two separate functions, the first of which is the Operations Control Incident Centre (OCIC). This is the room from which British Airways will respond to any incident which has a serious effect on operations and enables command and control of any such incident to be isolated from the routine control of normal operations. The other function is the Emergency Procedures Information Centre (EPIC) which would be set up in the unfortunate event of an accident or serious incident involving a British Airways aircraft (or one operated by an airline which subscribes to the EPIC facilities). This would basically act as a communications focal point in the event of such an accident or incident and would be manned by trained volunteers as well as representatives from the Metropolitan Police and the Royal Air Force.

The Compass Centre also includes a full range of staff facilities.

Appendix I

British Airways Route Network

The extensive British Airways route network serves over 150 destinations in 69 countries and is based mainly on Heathrow where the airline accounts for some 45% of the scheduled passengers using the airport. A number of European and intercontinental destinations are also served from other UK airports, notably Gatwick, where activity has expanded greatly in recent years, particularly following the take-over of CityFlyer Express, with the result that BA now occupies some 60% of the landing slots. A complete list of destinations served by flights from UK airports and based on the summer 1999 timetable is given below. Figures for the previous edition of this book (1997) are given in parentheses.

London Heathrow
Scheduled destinations served by *direct* flights with British Airways flight numbers. Many other destinations such as Durban, Sydney, Melbourne and San Diego are served by flights making one stopover.

Aberdeen	Bombay	Frankfurt	Manchester	Rome
Abu Dhabi	Bordeaux	Geneva	Mexico City	San Francisco
Adelaide	Boston	Glasgow	Miami	Seattle
Albany	Brussels	Hamburg	Milan (Linate)	Singapore
Almaty	Budapest	Hanover	Milan (Malpensa)	Stockholm
Amman	Cairo	Helsinki	Montreal	Stuttgart
Amsterdam	Calgary	Hong Kong	Moscow	Tehran
Anchorgae	Capetown	Istanbul	Munich	Tel Aviv
Athens	Chennai (Madras)	Jeddah	Newcastle	Tbilisi
Bahrain	Chicago	Jersey	New York (JFK)	Tokyo
Bangkok	Cologne	Johannesburg	New York	Toronto
Barbados	Copenhagen	Kuala Lumpur	(Newark)	Venice
Barcelona	Damascus	Kuwait	Nice	Vienna
Basle	Delhi	Lagos	Oslo	Warsaw
Beijing	Detroit	Larnaca	Ottowa	Washington
Beirut	Dhahran	Lisbon	Paris (CDG)	Yerevan
Belfast	Dubai	Los Angeles	Paris (Orly)	Zurich
Berlin	Dusseldorf	Luxembourg	Philadelphia	
Bilbao	Edinburgh	Lyon	Prague	
Bologna	Faro	Madrid	Riyadh	

Total destinations 96 (1997 — 123)

London Gatwick
Scheduled destinations served by direct flights with British Airways flight numbers.

Aberdeen	Charlotte	Harare	Moscow	Rotterdam
Abidjan	Cologne	Helsinki	Munich	St Petersburg
Accra	Cork	Houston	Murcia	São Paulo
Alicante	Dallas	Inverness	Nairobi	Seville
Amsterdam	Denver	Jersey	Naples	Sofia
Athens	Dhahran	Kingston	Nassau	Stockholm
Atlanta	Dublin	Krakow	Newcastle	Tampa
Baku	Dusseldorf	Kiev	Newquay	Tangier
Baltimore	Edinburgh	Lagos	New York (JFK)	Tel Aviv

Barbados	Faro	Lisbon	Nice	Toulouse
Barcelona	Florence/Pisa	Ljubljana	Oporto	Trieste
Belgrade	Frankfurt	Luxembourg	Orlando	Tunis
Bermuda	Funchal	Madrid	Oslo	Valencia
Bordeaux	Gdansk	Malaga	Palma	Verona
Bremen	Geneva	Malta	Paris (CDG)	Vienna
Brussels	Genoa	Manchester	Phoenix	Vilnius
Bucharest	Gibraltar	Marrakech	Pittsburgh	Washington
Budapest	Glasgow	Mauritius	Plymouth	Zagreb
Buenos Aires	Gothenburg	Miami	Riga	Zurich
Cancun	Guernsey	Milan (Malpensa)	Rio de Janeiro	
Caracas	Hamburg	Montpellier	Rome	

Total destinations 103 (1997 — 80)

Manchester
Scheduled destinations

Aberdeen	Cork	Glasgow	London	Paris (CDG)
Amsterdam	Dubai	Guernsey	(Heathrow)	Rome
Belfast (City)	Dublin	Hanover	Londonderry	Shannon
Belfast (Int)	Dusseldorf	Islamabad	Madrid	Southampton
Berlin	Edinburgh	Jersey	Milan	Stockholm
Billund	Frankfurt	Knock	Munich	Warsaw
Bristol	Geneva	London	New York (JFK)	Waterford
Brussels	Gibraltar	(Gatwick)	Oslo	

Total destinations 37 (1997 — 29)

Birmingham
Scheduled destinations

Aberdeen	Brussels	Frankfurt	Madrid	Paris (CDG)
Amsterdam	Copenhagen	Geneva	Malaga	Stuttgart
Barcelona	Dublin	Glasgow	Milan (Linate)	Vienna
Belfast	Dusseldorf	Hanover	Munich	
Berlin	Edinburgh	Lyon	Newcastle	

Total destinations 23 (1997 — 21)

Glasgow
Scheduled destinations

Aberdeen	Benbecula	Cardiff	London (Gatwick)	Stornoway
Barra	Birmingham	Inverness	Londonderry	Tiree
Belfast (City)	Bristol	Islay	Manchester	
Belfast (Int)	Campbeltown	London (Heathrow)	Southampton	

Total Destinations: 18 (1997 — 19)

Note: The above lists apply to British Airways scheduled flights, including destinations served by associated British Airways companies and code-sharing airlines.

Appendix II

FACTS AND FIGURES (Year to 31 March in each case)

1. BA Mainline Scheduled Services

	1999	1998	1997	1996	1995
Revenue passenger km (m)	118,310	106,739	102,304	96,163	87,395
Available seat km (m)	167,265	149,659	139,789	130,286	122,063
Passenger load factor (%)	70.7	71.3	73.2	73.8	71.6
Cargo tonne km (m)	4,277	4,181	3,790	3,476	3,349
Passengers carried (000)	37,090	34,377	33,440	32,272	30,552
Cargo tonnes carried (000)	855	816	721	672	666

Note: (m)=1 million

2. BA Group Operations (including Deutsche BA and TAT European)

	1999	1998	1997	1996	1995
Passengers carried (000)	45,049	40,955	38,180	36,003	35,643
Average total staff	64,051	60,770	59,218	56,720	54,958
Aircraft in service	335	330	308	293	283
A/c utilisation (hr/day)	8.71	8.48	8.46	8.28	8.20

3. British Airways Staff Numbers (as at 31 March 1998)

Mainline Operations

Pilots and co-pilots	3,285
Flight engineers	293
Cabin crew	14,864 (including 218 support cabin crew)
Maintenance and overhaul staff	8,628
Ticketing, sales and promotions staff	5,488
All other personnel	22,272
Total	**54,830**

TOP TEN WORLD AIRLINES — COMPARATIVE DATA 1998

Airline	RPKs (000,000s)	Total Pax (000s)	FTKs (000s)
1. United	201,715	79,733*	3,290,620*
2. American	180,144	75,862*	2,286,726*
3. Delta	168,596	97,294*	1,818,566*
4. Northwest	119,337	50,388*	2,735,601*
5. British Airways	**112,029**	**39,923**	**4,488,000**
6. Continental	96,580	40,428*	1,006,085*
7. Lufthansa	81,401	38,872	1,745,000
8. US Airways	66,738	57,527*	285,541*
9. Singapore	64,528	13,545	5,481,708
10. Southwest	58,695	60,066*	92,722*

RPK — Revenue Passenger Kilometres. FTK — Freight Tonnes Kilometres.

*Figures Jan-Nov 1999

Source: *Air Transport World*

Appendix III

British Airways on the Internet

In this age of global instant electronic communications, no self-respecting organisation can afford to be without an Internet web site. British Airways has one of the world's most advanced sites which is constantly being expanded. Apart from general information and timetables, potential passengers can make enquiries as well as book and pay for flights. The site is a mine of information about the airline and has an excellent site index listing literally hundreds of pages. There are detailed descriptions of each aircraft in the fleet, together with photographs and drawings. Concorde is given a sub-site of its own with a virtual reality tour. Details of various subsidiary and franchise airlines are given below, together with the necessary links.

www.britishairways.com	British Airways Official Web Site
www.go-fly.com	Go Fly Ltd
www.fly.to/cityflyer.com	CityFlyer
www.deutsche-ba.de	Deutsche BA

Accessing the following sites will take the browser directly to the appropriate page on British Airways' main site.

www.british-regional.com	British Regional Airlines
www.maersk-air.ltd.uk	Maersk Air UK
www.comair.co.za	Comair

In addition to these commercial sites, there are a number of sites run by enthusiasts which give detailed information on various aspects of the British Airways fleet. Among these are the following:

www.avnclub.demon.co.uk/   British Airways Aviation Section.
An excellent site run by a BA staff member giving a wealth of detail, particularly in respect of the Utopia tail images.

http://ourworld.compuserve.com/homepages/mikebarth/index.htm
Another enthusiasts' site run by Manchester-based Mike Barth who also provided many photos for this book. Gives fleet listings, many photographs of aircraft and close-ups of the World Images.

http://www.geocities.com/CapeCanaveral/Launchpad/2970/ UK and Ireland Fleet Listings. A constantly updated site which, as its title implies, covers UK and Irish Airlines. British Airways is fully covered, as are the various subsidiaries and franchise operators.